Measures of Me

Measures of Me

Carlton M. Bass

authorHOUSE®

AuthorHouse™ LLC
1663 Liberty Drive
Bloomington, IN 47403
www.authorhouse.com
Phone: 1-800-839-8640

Published by AuthorHouse   11/11/2013

ISBN: 978-1-4918-1672-1 (sc)
ISBN: 978-1-4918-1670-7 (hc)
ISBN: 978-1-4918-1671-4 (e)

Library of Congress Control Number: 2013917013

Contents

On My Own 2 1

It's Not Easy 2

Goodnight 3

1 ON 1 4

Spread the Word.. 5

Come Here 6

Look Outside 7

Different Lines 4 Different Times.. 8

Look At My Angel.. 10

Live Forever.. 11

Know the Difference 12

Love from Above 13

Last Night.. 14

Game Time 15

A Magical Night.. 16

Poetry.. 17

Be a Leader... 18

My Father, My Friend 19

I Say No More.. 20

Follow Me.. 21

Read This... 22

Untitled.. 23

I Wrote It in the Wind 24

Born Identity... 25

Days of the Week 26

It's More Than What It Is 27

Disturb the Peace 28

Eye Glasses 29

I'll Tell You If You Listen 30

So 4 real 31

Star Search 32

What I Told Her 33

Words of Strength 34

Food 4 Thought 35

Skyline 36

Until the Clock Strikes 37

Writing until Next Time 38

Descending 39

I'm just a Black Man 40

I'm Just Saying 41

True as Me 42

Seek and Receive 43

2 Whom It May concern 44

Take Your Time 45

Listen Close 46

Down the River 47

Facts of Life 48

2 My Father 49

Across the Ocean 50

Runway 51

Fresh Breath 52

My Birth, My Earth 53

Eraser 54

Hanging Around 55

Dear Mother 56

Speech Class 57

Unthaw Me 58

Rocking Chair 59

Sound Off 60

Refresh 61

Dance the Night Away 62

Complete Me 63

Witness Me 64

State farm 65

Untitled 66

Goldmine 67

Untitled 68

Praying for Myself 69

Let it Shine 70

From God 71

"Word Up" 72

The Truth Is 73

Fireplace 74

Born 2 Be 75

Supernatural 76

Study Hall 77

Untitled 78

If U Believe 79

ACHIEVABLE 80

Here I Am 81

So Much 2 Say 82

Here I Stand 83

My Prayer 84

Patiently Waiting 85

Gift Wrap 86

Live and Learn 87

Confessions 88

Ask and You Shall Receive 89

Eternal 90

Untitled... 91
Wonderland 92
Living Authority... 93
Don't Sweat It 94
I Know... 95
Perfect Match 96
Keep On Still 97
Untitled... 98
Smile... 99
Skyscraper 100
Keep Going.. 101
Feel Me 102
Untitled... 103
Closing Remarks 104
Falling from the Sky... 105
Love Me 106
Untitled... 107
Untitled... 108
Artistic 109
King... 110
Art Gallery 111
Untitled... 112
Day Dream 113
KO 114
Rose Garden... 115
Write.. 116
As We Dance.. 117
Air Fill... 118
Listen 119
Emerging 120
Wordsmith... 121
On my Way.. 122

Reason Being..123

Dial Tone 124

Untitled..125

Sorcerer 126

Young and Restless 127

The river that's in me 128

Below Deep..129

What is poetry? 130

Moving Along 131

Point Blank 132

Ringtone..133

Miracle on Westmont Street 134

Poetic Faith 135

Laying on Sheets 136

To the Future I Go 137

My Mental, Physical Life..138

Natural Reaction 139

Never Absent, but Always Present 140

Defense 141

Run with Me..142

From Scratch..143

Blessed 144

I'm Alive..145

A Whisper Said 146

Moments are like 147

Emancipated 148

Saving Account 149

I Still Write 150

I dedicate this book to my Lord that dwells in Me, I'm so grateful and excited at the same time for all you've done and still doing in my life! Also I'll like to dedicate this book to all my sisters and brothers who've passed away, the ones who dreams was never seen, the ones who cries was unheard and tears wasn't wiped, together right now we all shine through love of expressions! Follow what's in your heart, anything else would be uncivilized!

On My Own 2

I have thoughts on top of thoughts
Some buried away, some talk to me daily
I live off how experiences grade me, but I'm not failing,
just sailing across my imagination and stopping on occasions
I just try to be better than who I was yesterday
Look like the older you get the more you pray
Time make things look different most times
I'm growing and counting, adding up more rhymes
This is how I relieve pressure off my mind
Life priceless and love don't cost a dime
Won't too much change if I press rewind
You'll see moments of who I already was being defined
I'm not green by any mean but I am a GIANT!
I'm similar to the king of the jungle, the lion
I don't mean to harm, but only to hunt for the things I want
Life too short for me to ignore my dreams
I chase with precision and guidance from the Supreme
I'll forever be me when you see or when I'm not being seen
I'm living off how I feel and in my mind I'm a King
I don't need the world to tell me that, it's in my genes
When I write I hope you feel my energy
Deep down pass my eye site is my inner peace
I write it across these sheets from feelings held deep
and unleash at times I choose to write my speech
Life is a like a school and I was born to teach
Born to rule, born to BE
Don't look at me like I don't know who I am
I'm the TRUTH over any scam
My PRAYERS strong enough to get me out of any jam
And my mother taught me how to say, "Yes sir and Yes Ma'am"!
I want the same respect when my children calling
I'll share with them how all these words kept me from falling

It's Not Easy

It's not easy when being the name behind the blame
My own kind points a finger at me and the world does the same
I be feeling alone with thoughts of pain, then my eyes start to rain
I appear to be a magnet for problems while my spirit carries great fame
They stereo type me into a thug, but if you look close you'll see a man
needing a hug
Being a negative thought rips me apart, especially when they don't know
your heart
They have no idea of who I'm going to become, but I'll remember where
I came from
This drama really makes me strong, I can feel my inner strength holding on
Life a maze, you wake up being hazed by putting up with people and
their different ways
The result of it is mistreatment and from the world its impeachment
So I'm trying my best holding on to confidence while showing you my
real upper strength
I'm trying to over stand biology and my brain is more advanced than
technology
I'll continue to live this life not cheesing, I'm a grown man knowing it's
not easy

Goodnight

Take a dive inside my mind because thoughts are deep
You can swim around in my head since I write more than I sleep
I have no time to rest, I just make time for GOD so I can do things at
my best
I'll let my knowledge fly west and travel my lessons back east
I'll get the rest I deserve when I'm resting in peace
But peace don't exist, I'm trying to fight the power by placing a pen
between my finger and thumb of my fist
I'm going to confront devils from now until the very end
And if they swing back, I'll whip them with this pen
I haven't committed a foul act they just design a life for me to sin
Telling me I was wrong when I was right
Telling to be calm when I was supposed to fight
They tried to teach me how to love their wealth and hate myself
This King looked in the mirror and said they better play with somebody else
My mind is similar to gold and I recognized them trying to control me
when they was already out of control
So let me turn off their lights and let the black days be back bright
Never again will they be able to intercept our rights
I introduce devils to their death beds as I write
And this poem says "Goodnight"!

1 ON 1

Carlton—Excuse me but may I have some of your time?
Poetree—Only if you can present what's on your mind in a rhyme
Carlton—I'm not the poet who can make a poem rhyme every time
I brought this conversation to your attention because I admire the way
you made your own light shine
Poetree—Thank you my brother, I just was tired of taking advice from
people in the world who was blind
They was telling me the truth in their eyes, but we don't see eye to eye so
I saw them lying
I started searching for the truth even though inside I was crying
Carlton—So you felt bad for trying?
Poetree—No, I felt bad because up to now my mind was frying
I learned to take it easy because life don't suppose to be hard
We just keep catching hell because inside our decision making we don't
involve GOD
Carlton—You have so much to say about problems of today
Poetree—The way life was explained to us has us bringing problems
our way
We need to believe in ourselves and be sincere when we pray
Carlton—Thanks Poetree, I've learned so much within your lines
Poetree—You welcome brother because I'll always send knowledge
within my rhymes
Carlton—Well you out did yourself this time
Poetree—No I didn't because I'm not done
I was just having a conversation with you 1 on 1

Spread the Word

If you look past my art, you'll see a picture of a child with a broken heart
My heart is broken because my life was cursed from the start
I came out the womb looking for light,
but I'm still in the dark
I wasn't blind my vision was just wearing a scarf
Tell me who tried to cover the eyes of this beautiful star
Somebody knew who I was before me and in life they didn't want me to
make it far
My back was turned when I got cut now in life I just wear a scar
I can't forget what happened in my past because my past makes me the
man I am today
I'm a King without being acknowledge as one because my culture was
raped
And that fact is still absent from a mind of a child who's black
He or she doesn't know it since the history book of the educational
system didn't tell them that
I laced my poetry with knowledge and I feel like my teacher skills can
get us back on track
If you ever take the time to find out who you really are,
you wouldn't turn the other cheek, you'll attack you
Just tell me what's peaceful about how they treat us
Its hell for black males and politicians are acting like they're righteous
leaders
I can't wait to see these devils life catch a physical fever
They have no idea on when it'll take place because they can't read us
They'll comprehend it much better when each of us starts walking the
earth like Jesus!

Come Here

Read my pain and watch how I went through a spiritual changed
GOD warned my mind to expect evil play from a game, but no rules
was explained
Lost was a word I became so I told my eyes to let it rain
People look at me like I'm famous, but they eyes can't see my fame
They notice my potential and just look at me strange
They just looking at a sane man gone insane
My heart is not stable in my chest so I let it hang
My emotions has been on a roller coaster now I don't feel any joy and
my back is up against the wall like a poster
Don't expect me to keep standing still
My poems are letters from GOD to you and when I'm finished writing
my distance to him become closer
I'm smiling while I stare at the sky showing nature I want to get to know her
I use to look at my poetry and be unsure
Now I can look at my poetry and see a spiritual boy showing he's
becoming mature
When your eyes start leaking I bet I can make your pupils clear
If the government was able to see what is going on in my mind I'll be an
individual they fear
My poetry equals up to separate angels asking a lost soul to come near
Let me have your attention because GOD is telling you to come here!

Look Outside

Every time I run out of trouble I run in it
Not by choice, but by circumstances and I can't even comprehend it
The only thing I'm sure about is the amount of money I earn off my
poetry won't allow me to spend it
The royalty I deserve off each poem has multiplied from me writing so many
Do you think I'm trapped in crime or trapped in rhymes?
I believe I lived in both of these scenes from my eye sight of life and
visions from my mind
I'll speak my message from out the dark since I'm eager to shine
If you don't think I'm ready then clearly I think you're outside your mind
You see this life style belong to me and I'm just taking back what's mine
I have to use the vision I currently have to keep from going back blind
The changes I've been through changed me into a black man with a
huge amount of pride
I don't give 10% of my earnings off of green paper, but I still believe in
the message behind tithes
Faith has allowed me to make it this far even though I've been told
plenty of lies
The preacher lies, the female I slipped and fell in love with lied and the
government continues to lie
I'm speaking out right now because these are some of the ones who
ignored my pride
You shouldn't have lied to a King because us Kings don't forget lies
You'll never be able to set off another bomb in my world because I'm
disarming you from my eyes
You brought rain to my surface and then a rainbow appeared outside

*D*ifferent Lines 4 Different Times

I'm sitting in the dark with the sun in my eyes
I'm a soul child full of truth and I use my lethal vision to detect lies
Look at the vision I've painted with each of these black lives
It's a lonely wife in the bed lying next to a body full of lies
This husband is different from the character his wife dream of him to be
She accepts the life she has, but she know something is still missing inside
Now she's allowing love to think for her because she won't look for what it is
that's lost in her inner eyes
I hope she stand up because the truth she feel won't hide
Right now let me give a pat on the back of my little brother's pride
He's the oldest of five and the head of the household because his father died
So he's standing strong and respecting mother by learning on his own to
provide
He's the bodyguard of his sisters so they always feel protected
So many young men face this image or one similar to it and they should be
respected
It's another mother out there who hardly can stand on her feet
She just trying to stand strong after receiving news of her son being shot
down in these ruthless streets
Her only child is gone from raw beef being cooked with heat
She can't digest no justification for her son's murder so at night she can't sleep

It's a cold world even for this beautiful young girl
She's erratic so she can't stay calm, but she's also pregnant and don't know how to tell her mom
I guess she bit the cookie from having a sweet tooth but homie left a specific piece of crumb
I just hope this seed from a hot night don't get trapped in any traps of an uncle tom
They're after our babies and the males seem to be their favorite
Life is a gift that has left some unsatisfied
I think it's from the plan of the leprosy man who followed directions of how to conquer and divide
Now we trying to reverse things but each step is a long stride
You need to learn how to take your own steps so you can acknowledge when the blind is leading the blind
Some think it's the end, but I think it's the beginning of time
The visions I've painted within these lines won't be replayed in the era of a redeemed mankind

Look At My Angel

I'm looking at this paper trying to figure out the subject I need to
carry with this pen
I think I need to write about this beautiful woman who's also my
dear friend
I continue to get her wet from my storm and she don't frown up at
me she just grin
I know my looks might be a plus but she also really like my
individuality I carry within
I'm just thankful to have her as a friend so my pen and paper won't
be my only ones
I'm able to share secrets with her as well because I think our
friendship was premeditated at a well
I'm scared to fall in love with her from the fact me knowing her love
is a spell
Not one to cause me any harm just one where I know the love in it is
warm
My heart stays cold so you would think I would welcome her with
open arms
I still welcome her even though my arms aren't always open
I open them when I give her a hug because the love GOD placed
inside me is a token
I can't commit to her because overall my heart is still broken and
she's the fulfillment of expectations I had for a female who had my
past smoking
I don't live in the past because my friend I have near me pats me on
the back when I'm choking
Thank you for helping me out when I feel like I'm being strangled
I was created in God's image so you must be my angel

Live Forever

I'm writing this poem trying my best not to cry
I feel lonely like a tear in one eye
I'm just walking through a mental storm waiting on the surface to dry
God I need help exercising golden thoughts so I can see a sun in my sky
I know this breath of life wasn't given to me to think of ways to die
These suicidal thoughts can't be by my side because my pride won't
entertain thoughts of suicide
My worries is somebody else reality and if I can't divide my poetry up
into books I'm going to die inside of me
I refuse to faint off the letters that spell can't
My poetry is art so my life must be the paint
There is no such thing as a word called can't
Anything is possible with GOD and you can take that to the bank
I don't need materialistic fortune because I'm already rich from his love
All these sophisticated computers they keep building only do what my
brain does
They'll never be able to see what's on my mind
All they can do is read my poems and see how I kept upgrading my
rhymes
My knowledge keep growing and it's scary because I'm already ahead of
my time
My faith is teaching me how to live without the dime
Life is not about how much money you make while you living
It's about renewing your mind inside this GOD given time
There is no such thing as life without help from the spirit that's Divine
I found GOD behind the physical world and that discovery make my
wisdom rhyme
And my purpose is to write it down so I can live even when I'm dying

now the Difference

I'm still trying to learn the facts of life
We go through struggles because we never learn the first lesson right
Then a trend of things begin from things being done without sight
It's easy to become blind when you don't know the day from night
We already was born in an upside down world were evil people get
treated right
The humble ones deserve the best but instead they get treated below nice
The rich man is too rich and the poor man heart is like a cube of ice
They want you to smile when they doing you wrong so you can feel like
they doing you right
Everything is never what it seem and some people don't believe in having
dreams
I'm thinking twice when I'm in any scene
I was born in a dirty world and I'm living to be clean
It's hard to wash off this madness because you have to work for filthy
green
All money is dirty if you really know what I mean
It was the offered reward to take Jesus off the scene
Now everybody playing the role of Justus, selling their souls for a piece
of paper that's green
I don't understand why people turn to the devil if God's love doesn't cost
a thing
They must be ignorant to that fact or simply an ungrateful human being
How much more turmoil have to take place for people to see they can't
serve two Kings
I guess their living for the moment, but I'm living to be here after these
present things
In my eyes GOD is the only King
The devil can show you how to live fast but only GOD can show what
life really mean

Love from Above

I'm anxious to make my future present because I've grown so much from
my past
I disappeared from others vision just so they could see my dark years
wouldn't last
I lost my mind during this time but kept finding GOD inside my
rhymes
I'm thinking my way out this maze because my poetry is too bright not
to shine
I'm praying to keep my actions honest since I know my Father is Divine
I'm living my life honoring him so the devil won't try to control my mind
Discipline is a word I'm using for motivation while I'm passing
through time
War is all around me but my combat training don't have me with
thoughts of dying
GOD is raising me so I'm thinking eventually everything will be just fine
And if I don't think it who will? And I can't cry over milk that's
already spilled
I face a new day in a new way
I'm doing things off of answers I get back after I pray
Different actions bring different results so I won't do the same thing I
did yesterday
My past is full of sorrow, I found GOD from that frown now I'm living
for 2morrow
I'm writing down love you can have so it won't be something you have to
borrow
Just interpret the message I get from the MOST HIGH because he
always talking to the ones feeling low

ast Night

Last night I had a dream
Inside this fantasy world I met my Beautiful Queen
The woman I saw would've attracted my eyes in any scene
A sexy woman looking all mean, her coke bottle shape almost made me sing
So I pinched myself to see if this was the real thing
The love I felt for this woman could've been shown with a ring
I'll normally stay away from that subject but she had potential to be my
soul mate so scratch that
I introduced myself hoping to find out if her individuality matched
everything else
I walked up to her, but her beauty paralyzed my words so I just played it
off and asked for some help
She replied, how can I help you? And I said from the words your create
from your breath
She said excuse me and I asked could she spend her spare time with me
And she responded with I don't know we'll have to see
My seduction was my introduction and I responded back with I agree
We exchanged numbers so we could arrange a day to meet
After she left my sight, I knew to myself I couldn't leave her in my past
I went to the gas station that same night to get some potato chips but
she was actually pumping gas
We made eye contact and smiled at each other real fast
I walked up to her ride and asked if she'll join me on the riverfront by
my side
She couldn't answer me straight back because she was so surprised
She was silent a few more seconds, but she already said yes to my
question with her eyes
So she followed me to the destination
And I could tell she spent time in the hood because she set down in the
grass with no hesitation
I set down right beside her, looking at the flow of the river while I was
puffing off my medication
Afterwards she laying up under me saying if I fall asleep in your arms
that'll be something else
We fell asleep together, but I woke up by myself

Game Time

I'm trying to cry but this tear is stuck
My life feels like a pair of dice without the luck
My situations never work out
How can two dice add up to crapping out?
I was born in a wrestling match with the devil choking me and I feel like
tapping out
My personal angel whispered be strong because quitters don't have a
home
I'm not quitting, I just don't know where I belong
Which way to go, what daily activities should I do less and which ones
should be done more?
It's hard to decide when pregnant decisions are by your side
They're just giving birth to choices you must make with or without your
pride
I communicate with GOD at night so daily non-sense and knowledge of
mines can collide
I might not have an army behind me but I'm large in size
I been in the game using my poetry as a ladder to climb toward the top
I can see myself making it because I have the power to make the devil's
bed rock
Noticed my life has changed, even inside this poem I write out the
change
I changed my future into a sun from rain now I have joy instead of pain
And I've became The Game!

A Magical Night

It's a cool night, the wind is calm and the moon is bright
A young man is sitting on a bench in the park wishing GOD was in his sight
I guess he wanted to talk to the King of Kings, you know the author of the whole scene
This young man sitting on the bench mouth was shut, but his heart wanted to scream
He's angry at the world and the only companies his eyes can detect are tears
So he walked up to the pond looking at the reflection of the stars without knowing GOD was near
So he shouts out "Father, why do my pupils always have to look out of water?"
He felt the wind blowing and heard of a voice telling his heart "Don't question your father!"
The young man is thinking to himself things isn't getting any easier they're getting harder
He wanted his pain to vanish but he felt it so regularly he has to ask why bother
His eyes are asking the water, why I wear a frown instead of a crown?
His heart started to feel heavy in his chest and he noticed the Holy Spirit was around
Leaves started blowing off trees slapping him in the face and dropping him to his knees
He shouts out "God why are you punching me with your unseen breeze?"
A voice responded from over the trees because you're questioning the unseen King
I'm just molding you to be tough and I hear your cry so watch what I'll bring
Joy will knock on your door the pain you'll feel will be the unique awareness of not feeling bitter no more
I'm giving you a story to tell and when I'm finish with you, you'll tell it well
Poetree, I'm just making your poetry a spell
You drew your life in an art without allowing anyone to paint it
You just a seed starting to grow from being planted inside a time that was Ancient!
Sequel to "The Voice I Heard" from vol. 1

oetry

I'm still walking through a storm but the rain add to my change
The wind gives me visions of better weather while the thunder lifts the
power of my brain
My faith has grown dramatically through lost years of pain
I know God loves me and that fact alone help me to maintain
I read a lot because knowledge keeps my head full so my awareness won't
feel the presence of shame
I find myself to be a key player in this game and I dislike attention but
my heart know I deserve fame
I'm a Holy Poet and know it so I made Poetry my name
I was lost in the picture until I created myself in my own art and I titled
myself Poetry because that literature was my spiritual start
Who noticed my lonely dark nights when I was crying out to God?
Nobody, I witnessed those moments by myself while my mind carried
thoughts of life being too hard
I was moving slow but thinking fast, I started moving fast and thinking
slow
Then my pain disappeared in my past
My mind was empty until GOD gave my conscience gas
Now I'm thinking past the physical world looking for Heaven knowing
knowledge will handle that task

Say "Hello to Poetree", the spiritual son of Carlton Mashaun Bass

Be a Leader

My life reflects my heart, I been pumping up's and downs from the start
Sometimes my mind looks like the sky when it's blue
I locate gray clouds with my vision and when the rain comes the scene is
nothing new
I just have to carefully walk through the storm and remain true
I'm stepping out on faith showing others I can walk alone
Before I lose my whole family I'll make the streets my home
I have to help the future before it's gone so in other words I'm reaching
out to children who's alone
They growing up inside a foul scene
These devils have my brothers and sisters trying out for their team
At times living inside this system force us to do ungodly things
They dealt us our hand while looking at our cards to make sure we'll
never ourselves as Kings and Queens
Martin Luther had a dream and Malcolm X said by any means
Our mentality is divided and we haven't united as one because some
don't know the spirit within them is supreme
I'm going to let the children know the future is the manifestation of their
dreams
So pay attention to every child you see in your sight and I don't care how
you may do things but when that child watching you make sure your
actions is right

My Father, My Friend

Right now I'm writing without a cause because my mind always function
without a pause
So you'll never be able to stop what I think
My poetry is a chain reaction and I'm the responsible link
The vision I carry on paper don't blink
I'm just standing behind my words so my actions won't shrink
I'm a sleeping giant being disturbed and it's time for me to clean up the
dirt inside my world
My soul is too pure for me to be living filthy
I believe in magic because I can make a paralyzed mind feel me
I'm in touch with the spirit over man so you know my knowledge goes
real deep
Show me some love because I'm just a have not who represent the image
of a black sheep
I find myself to be born again, now I'm erasing sins with a pen
Look at how my positive thoughts turned my negative situation into a
moral win
I have the power to make enemies become friends
My mind was sitting still until God's wind blew and made it spend
And everything people told me about life, I had to question it again
God told me I created you to be a leader, not a follower and all the
answers you need are within
So we can take our secrets to God because he's our father and also a
friend

I Say No More

I'm not crazy about rain, but I love how I respond to a storm
Every time the devil tries to soak me with pain, I dry myself off with a poem
I learned not to panicked, I just let my faith rise above madness so I
won't sink like the Titanic
I won't allow myself to drown inside a pool of sin
I was born in God's image so in my eyes my life has no end
Jesus just wasn't my brother, but also my twin
My mind is a wheel of fortune that always spends
Maybe I'm speaking above your head and that's only because my poetic
thoughts come from God
I live every second of my life through him so we'll never be apart
In fact if you keep him on your mind you'll see life being easy instead of hard
It's time for you to rethink your thoughts because including God first is
the best way to start
I was lost in my life until I found a path to God through my heart
And I'm sure it's a path in yours, you just an individual like me who
trying to find Heaven's door
That's my only objective in life and nothing more
I want my steps to touchdown on God so in life I can score
And I been scoring every since I've been writing because I always send
waves of thoughts upon your mental shore
This poem is over because I say no more

Follow Me

I write with my heart so my thoughts always shine
I can't see how many souls I'll touch with words because my poetry is blind
I'm just trying to manifest my art into Godly work so it'll show up in
your dark days on time
All my thoughts are written in a fast forward motion so each poem can
display my life being rewind
I draw parables from mental images I have supplied in my mind
I'm a prophet inside my own rhymes because my spirit is Divine
That's a fact I use to be scared to speak
Now I'm on track writing down the truth because my pen carries heat
Burn baby burn, my objective is to put devils to sleep
The only way you can measure my knowledge is by saying that it's deep
They must have thought I couldn't fight since I'm a black sheep
Excuse me, they was wrong in the beginning because they tried to judge me
And my voice too strong for my opinions to be weak
My brother already defeated death so permanent sleep don't await thee
I'm Heaven bound and you can follow because the sign is ME!

ead This

Listen up so I can tell you about this lonely child who's stressed out but
continue to wear a smile
Nobody can locate his pain without committing a foul
How can he break up the fight that's within him when his thoughts
represent the crowd?
If I tell you about his broken heart, would you think he just broke it or
it was broken from the start
These issues aren't new because he always felt trapped
And when he speak out about his horror he feel like he's being slapped
Don't condemned him for his rebellious attitude since it's the reactions
of a lonely child who learned how to adapt
He's just living to learn so you won't consider him to be a boy in daddy's lap
His mind is much stronger than people realize it to be
So he has to wear a frown on the inside so he can smile while climbing
his poetry
That's the only time he really felt at peace, but when the pen drop the
war is back on
No more Divine time so he's back to feeling alone
When you read his poetry his love is always shown
Each poem exemplify how much this beautiful child has grown
And every time he call, God always pick up the phone
When he gets finish talking to him he always writes a poem
He's just exposing his obedience to God because the art of his poetry is
the picture from his storm
He sewed up his pain to keep his heart from feeling torn
It took a while for him to get his mind on track, but look at the seeds he
kept on sewing
Secret love letters to his generation and a generation that has yet to be born

Untitled

I'm not angry with nobody, but I still have an attitude
I've looked over bad choices of words that was spoken to me by other
people being rude
I guess they'll say I'm judging from my side, but to me they was
confused about being confused
I turned my back on senseless acts now everybody feels like I'm breaking
all the rules
I won't forget who stood on my side I'll rather forget the ones who
contributed to my blues
I withdrew myself from college, but inside my head I still went to school
If you feel like I'm talking for you inside my rhymes, then you right
because a lot of time I really do
God blessed me with that gift, but the secret won't be kept between me
and you
I'm writing down facts of me so the world can see I had nothing to lose
My story is so for real because life is so true
If I don't live out my purpose of being then I'll feel like I never did
anything about what I wanted to do
God granted me permission so now I must change my gray sky to blue
If I can write down tears during a storm then I can write down smiles
when the sun comes out too
Then I'll have my chance to be who I was supposed to be to you

Wrote It in the Wind

I'm writing a poem without knowing what to say
I wonder was this poem a thought predicted for this day
Maybe it was, maybe it wasn't
My poetry is a discussion about the truth without the fussing
I'm just writing down what I perceive through my eyes
You must understand the only way I can break the war up inside me is
by confronting lies
Every time I write I be in touch with this Divine spirit of mines
I thank God for it, I was born facing a struggle, but I'm proud of my
skin being black
And on top of that, I'm intelligent and wise so they can't hold me down
too long because eventually I'll rise
I'm trying to make every second my season and I don't write just to be
writing, I write for a reason
I don't speak it in them terms often because you can see it when you read me
I was born with a poetic spirit that allows my mind to touch other minds
in other regions
I know sometimes they be feeling like my words
Sometimes we are so concern with our own world that we don't be
noticing we share the same world
God is the father of the spirit and Mother Nature allow you to hear it
and we children of theirs
I didn't even know I'll write this when I picked up the pen
It's not hard to tell I wrote it in the wind

Born Identity

I been catching hell every since I placed the truth under my feet
Now I'm just walking through fire trying to learn how to ignore the heat
People look at me with a look that'll have me wondering what they see
I guess God has me glowing since my personality matches who I be
Every day I walk through a holy war but take every step in peace
I found myself living off faith because faith was living in me
I felt joy from making it through the storm
It was raining for a long time and you can tell by all these poems
I wrote enough answers for whoever wanted to ask me why
All my poems don't represent tears because sometimes I smile when I cry
I learned from my faults and the ground became dry
My pen is the telescope I used to look at the sky
I took away gray clouds when I was writing so you'll be able to see the
sunrise in my eyes
I was blind but now you can read about how I found my sight
I owe it all to God because he's my trainer through this fight
I owe it all to God because he's the unseen author when I write

Days of the Week

Monday, I see people having problems
Tuesday, I see people who can't solve them
Wednesday, I see people who feel bothered
Thursday, I saw a boy without a father
Friday, I told him he was in God's hand but it's up to him to work
harder
Saturday, I saw a girl eyes leaking water
Sunday, I told her to plant seeds with a good attitude so her faith could
grow taller
Monday, I don't know what happen, but dude got shot
Tuesday, I saw deadbeat dad making his baby mother hot
Wednesday, I mailed my heart out to them children who don't have any
food in their pot
Thursday, I noticed a family who miss grandmother a lot
Friday, I told some people they was slaves inside a system and they
looked back at me shocked
Saturday this expensive car got broken into even though the doors was
locked
Sunday, I said everybody praised God in some type of fashion, even a
rock
Monday, I said do the right things because you never know when your
breath will stop
Tuesday, I thanked God just for breathing
Wednesday, I prayed for them people who still are misleading
Thursday, I went outside and it was hot, but it supposed to be the winter
season
Friday, I said the only way you can see tomorrow is if today is see
through
Saturday, I said you can't judge time but some people try to
Sunday, I said the devil is all around because life has became lethal
These issues isn't just for the black race, they belong to people
Only the strong survive so don't play yourself or anybody else cheap
You must stand strong through each and every day of the week

It's More Than What It Is

My pops said "Get out!"
So I moved out on my own
My new surrounding is more peaceful, but I still feel alone
I know my mother miss my presence the most even though I'm grown
Now I'm standing on my own feet and even if I look weak, I'm healthy
and strong
Don't judge the cover of my book if you couldn't keep me calm on
nights that left me shook
When I was living blind everything was fine, but when I developed a
relationship with God everybody started treating me like a crook
I found vision through a lost look, but at the same time I felt doomed
You couldn't sweep away my pain even if I gave you a broom
And you can't stop me from being lonely even if we was in the same
room
I guess I'll feel heartbroken all the way up until it's time for me to bloom
I'm going to proposed during the right season so I can enjoy my
honeymoon
I'm sure some doubt my journey, but I'll find her soon
God is arranging a date for us to meet and I'm letting him organize it so
I won't have thoughts to cheat
I'll just live inside of love in case I don't wake up from my sleep
I'll wake up on the other side because life is deep

Disturb the Peace

I can't tell them what I see so I write down what I saw
I don't always trust ways of this modern day world so I just follow
wisdom from the Old Testament law
Some people disown the fact they addicted to meat, but the truth is too raw
My folks have ways of Romans and Greeks because they don't know
everything about what our ancestors taught
I'm an African without the American because America is just the land I
appeared on after my family members were caught
If they expected me to be proud of this country for that then I consider
their mind lost
I use common sense to come up with my opinions and I clashed with
ones who brain remain washed
Their minds be so closed to the point they actually think it's opened
Don't get too comfortable inside the matrix because the world around
you is still choking
Each day a different heart grow colder even if the sky is blue
A lot of people living a false life thinking it true
I write these poems to help myself and talk to the inner you
This my way of saying everything isn't what it seem and don't be fooled
Life is deeper than when you say life is deep
It's a reason behind every action and it's a miracle to breathe while you sleep
Some people look over simple things that count and some don't even
look to see
Cover up your nakedness with knowledge I continue to place on these sheets
I'm just writing how I feel about things even if it disturb the peace

Eye Glasses

I'm walking careful so I won't shake the ground with my heartbeat
I feel even more responsible now because I do have a mind to teach
When I'm not in your vision, I'm just some where updating my
knowledge so my actions can speak
People couldn't see what I was going through and that's why I write
down what the lesson taught me
This just the after math of a lost and found black man who thoughts
represent the struggle in the streets
Sometimes I feel separated from the reason why I breathe
I have to catch my breath from this tired world so I can take back the lead
Some live for today, but I live for tomorrow
I just write my poetry in a past tense mode so my path won't be hard to
follow
I give you a piece of my heart with every poem I write because the love
inside this world is hollow
So you'll never be able to live your life to the max because it's too many
other lives full of sorrow
My mind is ahead of time and that leaves my individuality to be unique,
simple, and deep
People look at me sometimes as if their mind was sleep
I just be wanting to know inside the stare how do they picture me?
I hope I'm not misunderstood because I always look to overstand
Locate the love inside me to see God because I'm just a man
Life is a gift that should always be adored and live out with a plan
You can't be productive if you confused about what's at hand
No worries, you won't be blind forever because I come to bring vision to
the land

I'll Tell You If You Listen

Time so precious but at the same time some aim to live reckless
I'm trying to live every minute because you can die in a second
You can either count on God or be controlled by the devil, but using
your first mind is always the correct method
You have to read the lines and everything in between because things isn't
what they seem
I woke up inside a nightmare from sleeping too long inside my dream
I'm just writing down my past because it's interesting how it disappeared
so fast
I saw it, but I didn't, heard sounds of chaos but refused to listen
Now I'm trying to last inside these days called the last
The world must be coming to some type of end when more people begin
to place their faith in cash
All this garbage around have some believing in trash
So I'm trying to help clean up this mess
Even when I lay down at night I never rest
I know I'm blessed but, it's still hard to live life ignoring stress
I guess that's the test of my faith or do our faith just be in a contest
I know we have the right answers behind our chest
Following your own knowledge will help every situation that was
helpless
It's more to life than comparing benefits from jobs
That's why poor people is rich in the eyes of God
You can't see it because you don't know about love
I'm not talking about that four letter word that you tell your significant
other every other day
I'm talking about that permanent love or should I say agape'?
The love that allowed the world to begin, the love that forgives sins, the
love that don't see the color of skin, the love that know the definition of
friend
The same love that guides my hand when I'm holding the pen

So 4 real

My life changed when I became a dark night inside a bright day
I saw a moon in my sky when everybody else had the sun shining in
their face
For the first time in my life I felt abandon and out of place
I became a lost child without knowing I'll give thanks to my exile
While I was wearing a frown God was wearing a smile
I actually thought I was in bad condition, but my spiritual awakening
was just telling me to learn things using my own intuition
I was a Muslim being raised like a Christian and you can't knock me
because I know God and the difference
I live through him so I can breathe through my poetic existence
Different nouns I use to like left my sight
I woke up when my old flame changed over night
I just think of her as gas for a fire that was already bright
Now I leave the paper smoking after I write
I inhaled God one time and was left high as a kite
I'm addicted to his love so in life the devil and I continue to fight
I'll digest him like lunch because each word I write is a powerful punch
My poems show I'm swinging all day long due to the fact I've written a
bunch
That's just how it is, I always write how I feel and my thoughts can't be
appealed
They'll help you like they helped me when I need a shield
So take heed to my lead because I'm so 4 real!

Star Search

They say life deep so I guess I'm at the bottom
If I panic I'll drown, but if I don't I'll find air to swallow
Now I'll have my chance to wake up to a better tomorrow
Honestly, I get tired of going to bed feeling sorrow
I'm too young to wear those emotions so I had to let my feelings go
Some knock my reality, but they'll respect the fact I'm living without a
shadow
My individuality and face has the same face
I'm going to be myself even if it leaves me feeling out of place
I'm just going to speak my opinions and walk away
You can argue with yourself as my distance become distant because I'm
from out of space
My mind is open to that fact, but yours might be a shut case
I'm similar to that star that normally shines during the day
In my world it's night time so every night I have to pray
I'm not trying to get caught up because I'm still catching up
This cold world can't answer any thoughtful question so you have to
repeat the comment "That's messed up!"
I'm lost in a scene that I consider to be wild
Too many single parent homes so we must turn back to the days when
the village raised the child
If each one teach one everybody can learn to smile, but it's too many
chips on shoulders so the majority wear a frown
We have to restore our faith by placing love on the ground
I'm trying to be around when Heaven on earth come back around
This poem is just a note from an instrument that hasn't been found
When the world find out about how my poetry stay on key they'll adore
my sound
Until then, I'll remain a diamond underground

What I Told Her

Let this sheet of paper be your hand and I'll let these words be mine
I'm bright as is, but baby you still make me shine
Such a good friend to me, so glad you don't be lying
A beautiful smile is all you need to wear
Your face shouldn't feel you crying
Gifts for you is what I'll like to be buying
I'm in the air from how my love for you be flying
Let me get behind your steering wheel and show you how I drive
I hope that picture wasn't too explicit for you, if so that was the wrong
slide, but how can I be wrong by complimenting your ride
I'm deep as the ocean, see me and dive
You won't drowned, you'll just float and look at the sky
If you ever see what I'm watching then you'll be in my eye
My vision is precision, I'm accurate as time
I'm on point because you on my mind
Take a walk with me and watch how I paint my rhymes
Baby you golden, you can't be measured by being a dime
That's like grabbing a lemon, but yet thinking about a lime
I know the difference and what became in time
I still love you, sweet lady of mine

Words of Strength

Brother to brother, man to man
I see your struggle homie, just do what you can
Whenever you think you lost the fight, just know the battle just begun
Too many frowns worn so that's why God is holding a day for us to have
some fun
It's all good, we already won
Path been laid, all we have to do is run through this jungle of time
Everything will be fine if we make that our motto to believe in
You can't let your ground be hollow when your patience wearing thin
You must gain control, calm down and don't place your faith in sin
Boys need to be boys and men need to be men
We must protect our mothers, sisters, and children because evil is
blowing in the wind
Cover your heart up, the devil trying to steal it from within, but he can't
withstand the presence of a man believing in GOD and knowing he can
We countless as the fibers of sand
Men of the Lord, powerful we stand
Thank GOD for the air you breathing, Amen!

Food 4 Thought

I write it like how it is
I'm a writer for real
Confessed emotions improve my skill
Life still seem like a big hill
The news still gave my body chills
I'm still treating this paper like oil using the pen to drill
Reality is a job that won't allow my dreams to spill
Judge me while I do what I feel
I'm trying to change the world I touch from thinking I will
Belief is essential if you want your outcome to live
Thoughts are more that what you think
They're seals of what you'll be
Enjoy the ride, but I hope you know the wheels isn't free
Look up and it'll be gone after your eyes open from a blink
You better think about what you thinking about and make sure your
actions make it complete
I know I'm winning because I'm not aiming at defeat
I know a lot of things and defeat doesn't know me
I owe too much to myself before I'll let that word owe me
I know the way to the truth, but I'll show you after I show me
Experiences show us what's bitter and sweet
I let my food for thought be things I like to eat

Skyline

I give it all on the paper
My emotions hanging like drapers
Too many blessings around me not to have God's favor
It's shout season in Heaven and I'm Jesus neighbor
My state of mind can't be located on cable
My favorite time is holding a pen and feeling able
My dream been in a wreck, but my condition is stable
I'm still creating poetry that's hard to label
I can't give up on what empowers me
Thoughts address me despite what the hour read
My inner peace is taking time out to conduct heat
It's a cold world and I need room to BE
I feel power in every step I take knowing love surrounds me
That notion dwells above my head and I'm thinking to believe in every
step I take
Day or night, I pray and fight for all my mistakes hoping they didn't cost
me inside life where living suppose to be free
I'm living to learn what's right or wrong inside my life hoping my fears
flee into the night
Tears drop inside the pen before I write
The hurt in my stomach eases up from being so tight
Reality is behind every word so check out my life
I'm showing how my expressions of thought became a sky for my night

Until the Clock Strikes

I'm running to the finish line holding a book of my rhymes
I'm low on dimes and the thought of me doing fine haven't crossed my mind
I keep seeing struggles growing on me like a vine
I see myself progressing then I go blind
It's like looking out the window seeing the sun then somebody close the blinds
I'm just trying to run in the direction I've placed inside my mind
I guess my watch be fast when I go to thinking it's my time
It's hard to relax I see too many questions marks outside
How can I concentrate knowing my patience and pride continue to collided?
What course I'm on?
God please don't leave my side
I drove too far to stop and let the devil drive
I wish love was a place where I could hide
My dreams so vivid, I see them passing by
New taste of life at the tip of my tongue, but my throat dry
Words are children of mine that I hate to see cry
Give me a break I always try after I try
I see the future in my sleep and I can't wait to wake up with it in my eye!
Lord please allow that time to come before I die

Writing until Next Time

I was born to die as is
Lord please show me how to live
Being rich isn't important, but yet I want to know how it feels
My desire is to live off my own skill
I been writing these poems like a drill
Success comes after you know it's real
I'm still looking around the corner anticipating what's coming by the
wind chill
I want my food for thoughts loud enough to smell
Your attention will support how I undress my life in detail
My words are letters from my heart to males and females
I don't discriminate, I relate to whoever felt what I wrote down
Ask me why I do it, well to study why I smile and frown
I stop painting the town every time I drop the pen from writing a poem
The world so cold because people don't know love is warm
I'm practicing ways of love before thoughts of hate can change the
outcome
I know I'm not the only one planting seed in this type of farm
I won't give up on that piece of land
I'll be there when it comes or wake up after it's done
Until then, I'll be writing on

Descending

Full moon outside
Thoughts won't hide
Fire bright from war inside
I'm about to open my door of eyes
The truth kills all types of lies
Love know what's wrong when a baby cries
I'm more peaceful than a group of guns inside a house of knives
Why did the men in the Bible have so many wives?
What role does that play inside my salvation?
I guess decisions always facing situations
I think vision is as important as dedication
How can you figure out what to do without a plan?
My mind looks like a bunch of ideas hitting a fan
I love my work more than any woman or man
My art so hot you might catch a tan
My heartbeat goes to the music of God's band
I believe my future was drawn by God's hand
I'm biblical and my knowledge carries a holy brand
I live off my own truth, I don't follow what people be saying
You need to learn about God yourself and that journey will take you to
praying
After I prayed, I found myself on the path of being enhanced
Runaway clear, dream about to land

I'm just a Black Man

I'm just a black man feeling like I have the world on my shoulders
I'm just a black man knowing each day the world get colder
I'm just a black man going to work every morning
I'm just a black man who watched over my son while he snoring
I'm just a black man who love his daughter for an enjoyment
I'm just a black man supporting my family like my father did
I'm just a black man who carried a broken heart as a kid
I'm just a black man who trying to lose weight because I'm too big
I'm just a black man learning how to cook something other than beef or
parts of a pig
I'm just a black man with dreams of becoming rich
I'm just a black man who likes to punch and kick
I'm just a black man who eat nothing, but vegetables and fish
I'm just a black man hoping God fulfill my wish
I'm just a black man looking for a hitch
I'm just a black man thinking to myself, life have to be more than this
I'm just a black man mourning over my mother knowing she'll be missed
I'm just a black man incarcerated waiting to be set free
I'm just a black man who gets high and looks in the mirror wondering if
that's me
I'm just a black man looking for peace
I'm just a black man who don't trust the police
I'm just a black man who know it hard being a black man
I'm just a black man asking God to hold my hand!

I'm Just Saying

I fight to win
I sit and watch the wind
Babies and old people make me grin
I'm my friend
Time has no end
Where the pen?
Oh snaps, in my hand
They don't understand
I wrote the whole plan
I know GOD over man
My thoughts grand
Life like quick sand
You better think fast
I'm in a trance
Words are advanced
They don't like what I'm saying
I'm going to keep praying
Obeying the voice inside
Emotions don't hide
Hoping gets me by
You can see pass me in my eye
Life don't die
Devil does lie
A miracle is the sky
Dreams fly left and right
They land when I write
I'm always in God's sight

True as Me

I'm living through moments that circle time inside my mind,
but everything is fine, well that's what I hope
Being a man isn't a joke, every second you learn how to cope with
whatever the problem seem to be
32 years old and I'm still learning about me with so much left
undiscovered
They'll never know who I was, in their eyes I'm just their brother,
but mother told me I was special or either that's just what my ears heard
or maybe the way I felt
Need a lot of help, but I dislike asking for help
I figure since God already know what's wrong with me who else do I
need to tell?
I have enough knowledge to speak over the head of any student
attending the University of Yale, but don't tell anybody my hobby was
preordained and every time I write I stop the rain inside my life
Whether its day or night I fight battles unseen by the human eye until I
write leaving the paper as my witness of me being present with thoughts
of Heaven
Lord let me just feel your blessing because they don't feel me and you
told me to be who I am and every moment feel like my turn
Tired of being the opposite of what was mention even though I hate
attention
Living from other standards over being a poet will have me feeling like
I'm in prison
Instead I'm free to exercise my vision of having sight without being
dizzy!

Seek and Receive

I have thoughts and thoughts and thoughts
I'm just trying to figure out what's true or false inside a world that's lost
and found
I been hounded by a fight that don't even carry rounds
I'm deep as the curves inside a frown
I'm just a King who haven't been crowned
I do things that still make some wonder how
My dream was organize from a place beyond the clouds
I let my imagination fly and it leaves me with a feeling of being proud
Open the deepest door inside your brain because that's where I'm at
knocking loud
I can't control time, but I can prepare myself during minutes to face each
hour
I jump in and out the gift and curse like a shower
I'm trying to be strong enough to control my own power
I wonder how sweet life can be after you taste it being sour
I'm still walking through a desert trying to spot a flower
It need to rain because this heat draining me out
My writings be paintings you have to hang upside down
Before you judge what you see, I hope you see how I smile
Lord knows that'll make me smile
It'll be like a young man having a NBA dream and draft day was now

2Whom It May concern

Lord show me the way because sometimes I truly don't know it
I can fix any situation, Lord I hope I don't blow it
Vision getting foggier each day, but I can't show it
I guess I suppose to see everything that comes up and down the road
Sometimes things show up in my face and I lose a level of control
Behold, I learn a day at a time even though days stay on my mind which
have me writing during the week when I'm feeling weak
I'll really like to see how it feels to be at a peak of success, not saying I'm
a failure, but at times I still wear stress
All I be doing is using a pen to show parts of me I consider to be my best
Any judgment of my life being done by anybody other than me need to rest
I'm not scared to confess any fault of mine
I'm not blind to things I see, me, or what I've done
Every time I drop the pen I feel like I won which mean no one can
control the happiness in me after my gift just happen and I keep
wrapping other ones up for other times
Leave me alone let me play with my mind
I'm just trying to figure out how to make my shadow shine since I refuse
to let darkness follow me
I just want to be ME inside every step I take
How can these thoughts be a mistake?
My poetry true as me on any day

Take Your Time

Please cover your eyes you might can't handle my shine
Please recognize I'm slightly ahead of my time
I'm a genius and I promise I'm not lying
If you see what's on my mind you'll be outside your mind
I write in time and live in rhymes
I know how to operate without having a penny, nickel, or dime
Love don't cost thing, but yet it's so valuable
All this love I have, how could you ignore what I do?
Piss poor and I'm still richer than the richest dude
My brain is an encyclopedia of time
Knowledge be mine, I'm Divine
You know I'm similar to a Giant, but you might not see me as that size
I'm taller than you think and impossible to shrink
I'll always be around because I have too many words floating around
Generations later will figure me out because I'm too deep for NOW
I can't sleep, thoughts ringing too loud
I need to lie down, but I'm already lying down
I don't want to slow down from thinking I haven't went fast enough
Lord holding me up in case weariness comes down
What's the value of joy when you learn how to smile from a frown?
I'm through with this one because that'll have you thinking for a while

Listen Close

I'm living today thinking about tomorrow
Tonight I need to pray about how I'll handle my sorrow
I'm still digging inside my potential wondering how far I'll go
Thoughts pop out the same way cannons blow
God be telling me yes when people be telling me no
Don't fast forward me, read everything slow
I promise you'll get a kick out of how much I know
No boasting inside my flow, I'm just sharing with you how God allow
me to soar
The world similar to a jungle and my poetry is similar to a lion's roar
King by a lot of means is what I place inside my head before I leave out
the door
Ideas serve as ammunition inside any war
I started writing because I couldn't handle times of being bored
People look at me without having knowledge of how much knowledge I
have stored inside my soul
My age doesn't tell you how old I am
I'm beyond time, I'm who I am everyday of the week doing things that'll
allow me to reap peace
I'm going to keep driving until I end up on sleeping street
In the mean time I'm writing notes from my heartbeat
This is how I let my art speak

Down the River

I can feel the wind blowing even though I'm inside
Thoughts born daily, vision look like a hill side
Take it easy is what I tell myself, but hard times won't hide
I see them around corners I drive and I holler out I'm just passing by
I can't stop and talk, it's too cold outside
I know some think I've changed, but if I didn't I'll still be behind
Changed come with time and I learned that as maturity started sitting
down in my mind
Some thoughts make me say wow! Besides me who would've thought I'll
be the way I am now?
My poetry look like me raising my eye brow
My personality so dominant that it had me apart of the in and out
crowd, but don't ask me how
I just keep living to answer every question that start with why or how
because I want to find out things I should know and things that'll make
me grow
My feelings be uncharacteristic like seeing snow in the summer time
I'll never let being dumb enter my mind
I'm too talented, I'm too wise
Confidence inside every step every since God made it out to be a guide
And I follow it thoroughly knowing it'll take me to high places from all
the faces I show
I threw my hand in so I'll glow
I don't half time my shine, I let it flow!

Facts of Life

Watch me close Lord, I need your guidance
Thoughts talk to me even when I'm silent
My wisdom allow my ways to be the opposite of violent
I'm just a vibrant individual still digging up my talent that was buried
beneath the sand
Now here I stand inside the days of being a man
I'm just walking with time holding on to values I found laying around
inside my mind
Holding a pen makes the time around me fine as a piece of thread
blowing in the wind
Time and time again I've experienced this time
The whole world is quiet when I'm writing my rhymes
My eyes be watering poems that grow in a vine
Lord knows my words stick together like seasons and time
I'm carrying ideas that could knock down a Giant
My art so defiant and my soul so Divine
My poetry is directions in life because each one is a sign
I follow my heart hoping the outcomes I walk through be kind, but
what's the reality of that?
Whatever you give life, life will give it back

2 My Father

When I have a family, I'll look forward to displaying my father ways
Cool, calm, collect and keep all the bills paid
He's been around since day one and played a part in how I was raised
I try to follow his footsteps but even I know one is hard to match
A man worthy enough to be praised but he wouldn't want all that
So I'll stay loving you as my father because you've always been that
I don't remember any lies being spoken from you or mother, just facts
And in this day in time it's hard to ask for that
So I'm grateful and excited to have your ways in me as a guided light
The world will never be dark because you still giving me insight along
with wisdom that continue to live
Father figure, man you something bigger than that for real
The picture drawn would be impossible for somebody to steal
Thank you for being the way you are because when I come around I give
people something to feel
A man with order makes people feel secure
I try to do right and place ways of being wrong in the rear
And that's how you taught me to be
Stand tall, never panic, and have no fear
Thank you for being my father each day of the year

Across the Ocean

Have you ever seen a man's life being trace by a pen?
My dream start where my finger tips end
Ink keep spilling over my emotions showing pictures from within
Now you see me for who I really am
And I'm more truthful than your Uncle Sam
I love everything that's not a scam
My goals are higher than the ones people try to slam
Excuse me for a moment and let me thank God for getting me out of
every jam I've ever been in
The past gone, but the present got me feeling like I'm born again
I keep writing because every now and then I feel torn again
I was a poet before I pick up the pen
My mind spend like the hands on clock
Thoughts fall like tear drops
I keep planting seeds hoping it'll rain on my crops
This became therapy after I fell in shocked from finding out the world
really dark
I turned the lights on in my area from looking at things through my
heart
Now every opportunity arise becomes me doing my part
I'm not old, but I do have old fashion art
My poetry navigates me around like a chart

unway

I'm inseparable from my thoughts
I'm impeccable from my faults
I look at the paper to review my past
Poet by nature is the scene under my lash
Notebook look like fiberglass
I'm hard to break and built to last
What I think of myself out values cash
Touched by God as I attend class
Life only hard when you do things fast
Slow down, you can't make up time
Be swift as if you being chased by a giant
My dreams don't occur at night, they take place while I'm alive
I'm breathing in your sight so ask God if I'm lying
All these words I write solves me like a crime
Should I feel guilty because I wear a shine?
I think not because I'm not blind
I'm fine from knowing who I am!
And feel even better being a part of the plan
In my mind I'm more than, but on earth I'm just a man
I don't walk nowhere by myself, God always holding my hand
How can I fail at anything when I'm the answer of it?
You can either love what I do or else judge it
I'm tough as nails, you don't know my substance
Just know I'm authentic inside any subject
I'm now landing from taking off like a jet!

Fresh Breath

I'm living like I woke up on the wrong side of the bed
The world keeps turning like the thoughts in my head
I'm yearning for understanding, but some things still be left unsaid
I have so much more to learn before I visit the word dead
I'm chasing dreams and taking chances without being scared
I'm the physical presentation of each and every word
Thoughts start at the top then crawl down my nerves
My biography come from a voice that's unheard by you until I write
down what it tell me to
If it's night time in my life this is how I turn the sky blue
Some think I'm a weird dude, but being perfect miss me by inches
How true am I?
True enough to admit when I lied
So many ways to be but that don't mean they'll be right
I'm still searching as I write to look for different combinations to help
me win this fight
Each day is a battle and each night I survive
Different mind states keep crowding my mind as I watch different
pictures from my eyes
Visions I see don't have me surprised, but some of them still burn my
eyes
Which answers belong to God, which ones mine?
I need to continue to grow and keep my eyes open wide
God show me things man couldn't even figure out
I wonder if my days are being affected from me being from the south
I'll keep living for answers as I breathe in and out

My Birth, My Earth

I woke up this morning grateful to have opened my eyes
Before I move a muscle I need to thank God for being alive
Life so precious, every day is a surprise
I cherish the moments I frown and smile knowing reality is a place I
can't escape
Let me tell you a secret, I'm superman without the cape
I'm beyond your beliefs of me, just ask my fate
My most frequent thought is "Devil get out my way!"
My path already laid and I'll walk in the sun or shade
Even if I'm broke or paid, love still surrounds my days
My poetic DNA allow me to stand up straight
I'm walking through opportunities passing the ones who told me to wait
I guess the things I'm trying to build wasn't on their mind to make
Belief came before what I did if you want the recipe to cook what I ate
Even if I stop writing, I'll still have words all over the place
My gift was given to me by God so it's not an object you can trace
Only God can judge me so I do things at my own pace
I can pick up my book and look at my own face
God wasn't good to me, he's been better than great
Whatever I ask him for, he say ok
He told me I could have the world as long as I do things his way, I said ok

raser

I don't know who these people thought I was
Some lost guy? Yea I was
I found God and things started adding up
I'm artistic without a brush
I'm breathing out my emotions from being crushed
The past got me feeling like I'm owed much
I'm not giving up, I'm just giving love
I'm peaceful like the sky above
I'm focus as a doctor performing surgery wearing gloves
Support allow you to feel like you receiving a well deserved hug
If you haven't heard, then I'll tell you now that it's unhealthy to hold a
grudge
Life too short to judge and God said be fruitful and go multiply and
now we doing all type of stuff
Love without meaning might be known as lust
I don't know it all, but what I know is a plus and far from enough
So my journey must continue on, I'm close and far from home
I couldn't tell you the answer if you asked what's wrong
I have too many answers for that one question now let's move along
Poet by blood, this isn't some fake calling
So many thoughts inside my room I could make the walls fall in
Then I'll have too much to clean up
I'll just keep evolving with time erasing my pain with love because God
is love!

Hanging Around

The moment turns special when I pick up the pen
Without it I'm just a brother dodging sins
Temptation makes it hard to concentrate on how to win
Just because I'm rolling a blunt don't mean my faith wearing thin
I'm maintaining as I take steps here on earth still being amazed by the
wind
I'm deep as the ocean, but don't dive in unless you ready to swim inside
this type of water
I was born from a struggle of knowing each day get harder
It's too late for sorrow, grounds I walk on be hollow
I'll look for myself before I try to find someone else to follow
Time move fast so that's why I look to live slowly
Judge others, hell no!
I barely have enough vision to watch my traffic
I'm simple, but life acrobatic, I write my expressions without being
dramatic
You won't see me often because I spend a lot of time in the attic,
thoughts erratic, but yet formatted
My imagination is gigantic and things I create from it is organic
Best results so far in my life came from me practicing who I thought I
was originally and practice make perfect eventually
I'm walking inside scenes I wrote down
Joy comes when you let your smile drown your frown
I'll be back soon, catch me on the rebound
Until then I'll be hanging around

Dear Mother

I'm trying to write you another poem thinking what could I say next?
My love for you is endless, never forget that
You taught me how to love, share, and respect
First teacher in my eyes, first person I ever met
You discipline me every time I was acting like I didn't know how to act
Now today I carry myself inside the mind state of knowing I was reared
up right
My gift to you comes from how I love to write
I told you I was going to have a book and look what God did, made me
right
Momma you shine bright as the stars in the sky at night
Pops made a great decision in making you his wife
After all, where would I be if you weren't in my life?
That's a scary thought because you was the first person I saw using my
sight
I wouldn't trade you for nothing inside or outside this world
You bought me cheese popcorn at school the following day to a night of
me rocking your nerves
What you've done for your children is beyond thinking of what you
deserve
That's why I write you these poems showing my love for you is reserved

Speech Class

First of all, let me thank God for turning my vision on
Thoughts all around my dome
I don't work out much, but I promise you I'm super strong, mind state
wise
Truth at heart, art paint no lies
Emotions full, I write from inside
Gravity inside my conscience, watch me glide or should I say float?
My faith is like a rope I'm hanging on to keep from falling below
Watch me pull myself up, watch me glow
I'm different from the last man you saw unless you just got finish
looking at a picture of me
And I don't take a lot of those during any day of the week
Man I'm so unique during each day of the week
Only the strong survive so don't picture me being weak
Picture me not knowing defeat
My thoughts and I don't clash, we meet
Blood running through my veins like a track meet
Colors can talk so I'm letting my black speak
So many police cars have my kind in the back seat
Everybody want a piece like we some meat
Never will I be messy, I'm neat
How do I look? I'm dressed in peace
Argue with whom? You can talk to me
I'll listen to you, just listen to me

Unthaw Me

I'm running with a purpose
World look like a circus
Wicked ways all over earth's crust
People do everything instead of love and trust
The only voice I follow is the one in my gut
All I see is what's outside from a door that's been shut
Here I go, like water watch me flow
Listen close, my tone often be low
I'm just drawing myself inside the show
You just now finding out but God already know
Things I'm facing was seen years ago
I have a grip on life so I can have control
Chip on my shoulder turned my attitude bold
All this hatred within the world has the weather cold
All this pain I feel has me feeling old
I'm young as the story being told
Ideas of mine remind me of bars of gold
I'm rich in mind, diamonds twinkle like my soul
I was born to shine, God is anticipating my glow
Grateful to know he keep waking me up every morning to do so
Plan in motion, poetry is the way to go
It gives me freedom inside things I know
Mind opened for visions to come and grow
I'm passing through time learning slow
The pen is my friend and we kick it when the wind blow
I captured the moment, my pictures froze

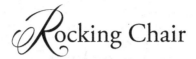ocking Chair

I'm just sitting in my rocking chair rocking back and forth wondering
where time went as I sit on the porch
I'm reminiscing about the honest fun I had as a little boy and how things
change once you grow up
The things that was hard to understand becomes self explanatory
They tell you about God as a kid, once you grow up you'll be looking for
his glory at some point in time
I'm just sitting in my rocking chair rocking back and forth thinking
about life in general and mines
The only way you can progress is by thanking God for the good and bad
times
And to study the lessons of what you learn during these moments
Life itself is untold because everybody life is different
Advice can and should be given, but it'll be useless if you don't know
where to apply it when time comes to spend it
Please pay attention to your inner voice and never make a race out of a
choice
Take your time you don't have to be in a rush
I'm just rocking in my rocking chair sitting on my porch hoping these
knuckle head boys don't grow up to deal or use drugs but Lord knows
certain circumstances make a child's life harder than anybody trying to
be tough
I just hope they keep their eyes on God inside these days of shoot outs
and clouds of dust
It be hard to cry sometimes, it be hard to trust
Keep God first, keep fighting and don't give up
If you need me you can find me sitting on my porch rocking in my
rocking chair back and forth!

Sound Off

They say it's a thin line between love and hate
It's a fine line between real and fake
Questioning my expressions is a mistake
My advice to you is love me and relate
I be moving this pen when it's late
If each poem is a leaf then I have too many to rake
Some days I have patience, some days I want to do everything but wait
Rushing won't help even though life seem like a big race
I just need God to cover me with his amazing grace
I'm writing down all these expressions off my face
I'm face down, but yet I'm standing up straight
Before I reach greatness I have to feel great
It's a cold world, but prayers allow me to feel safe
I been at it for a while, but it's still hard to see what I'm trying to make
Rest assure I see it clear as the sky when the sun hanging in the day
I try to be real as my actions matching what I say
Emotions of mine been up and down, but when their up I feel as if I'm
having my way
I know adversity is a part of life, but that won't ruin my day
All I have is what I think about and with it I'm ok
They say you can hear a wise man talking without him speaking, but if
you can't let me demonstrate
Each step I take I be a step away
My mind spend like the earth do day by day
This poem is heartfelt so I'll just let the beat play

efresh

Fear is a word, but sometimes I act as if it's a condition
Life change day by day so every night I go to bed wishing, hoping for a
better tomorrow
I'm not holding back, I already let go
My heart still beating as I walk through the smoke
No joke when I tell you I'm everything I wrote
And even if they don't see me for who I am, God still know who he
made me to be and even if they disagree
I must continue to show actions of how I think
I woke up this morning inside a long stare thinking to myself, I'm a
blink away from being ok
When doubt come around take a minute to pray
Sometimes the future look scary but right now I feel safe
I guess it's all the same when you live day by day
I'm just a simple man telling my story play by play
Glory goes to God everyday because it's a blessing to see the sky when
morning takes place
That's beautiful as me saying I love my race
I don't wear makeup, but I'm still trying to put love on my face
This world too cold, hope God warm up this place
I use my faith to picture the things I'm trying to make
God already gave me things man can't take
You know like love, joy, peace and grace
So this is what I do to refresh my memory
The first thing I notice when I wake up is that I can see
So God "Thank you" for allowing me to be!

Dance the Night Away

How can I be denied?
My gift is being applied
Tell pain bye
Tell joy hello
I trust God because love don't lie
Time fly through days and nights
And my age chase it like the words I write
I define these moments as my twilights
My skin black, but I'm too bright
Don't judge me, I'm too right
I'm not a helpless sheep, I will fight
At my wedding throw prayers over me instead of rice
Thoughts are far out when I'm holding the pen tight
My heart pours out when emotions are enticed
I be hugging the night with my insight
Everything I plant be in light
I'm an artist, my portraits be like one behind another
The air I breathe in is important like the sky above us
The air I breathe out tell me who to trust
I'm trying to make everything I do be a plus
I write from dusk to dawn and from dawn to dusk
I don't think my life happen by chance or luck
It was planned out a time in advanced
God, knowledge of mine please enhance
So I can continue to surround my heartbeat with music used for me to
dance

Complete Me

Life awaits me
The wind chases me
I'm just a lost dream hoping time find me
Every morning the birds sing
Thoughts run like a river stream
Mirror reflection show a King
I grow every second I breathe
God gave me life so I'm going to give life me
So much wisdom beneath my wings
Come fly with me
Let me show you the eye glasses that helps me see
I'm free as any leaf floating from a breeze
Death passes me every time I sneeze
God blesses me without me saying please
I'm too grateful is what I told him when I was praying on my knees
Poet at heart, all you have to do is listen or read
I place my verdicts all over these sheets
I need a tune up from how my love and pain leak
Life priceless, but some live cheap
All I want to do is what thrills me
Until then I'm incomplete
My drive is full speed in the street
I'm sowing seeds every day of the week
I'll be able to eat fruit off my own tree
God made me so how can somebody own me?
Everything makes sense when I think before I speak
Mission accomplished, poem complete

Witness Me

My emotions turn like a steering wheel
I search for what I feel
Knowledge is fruit I love to peel
Call me what you want, but I'm real
All I have is my thoughts and that's for real
We suppose to be one big family, but every day somebody get killed
Heartless as it sound, it still become what the news revealed
It's a cold world out here and it's raining down tears
God speak to me clearly as I face my fears
Nothing is automatic in life, you have to shift gears
I'm moving clockwise hoping God continue to direct me over the years
I looked my dream in the eye and said, "Come here!"
I'm walking toward the future as the present move into the rear
Pain don't last forever, one day I'll cheer for myself at a level I always
wanted to feel
Progression will allow that vision to be still
Then I'll witness moments of clarity
I give my love away for free, its charity
I have a positive and negative side like a battery
I try to stay positive so I can be included in God's will
Some act as if that's not a big deal
All I can do is watch the steps I take through the field
Adversity won't break me because I know what it is
My knowledge carries a lot of wonder years
Then they see me and assume my age under what it really is
I laugh at it all as I think to myself life weird, maybe I should grow a
beard
Instead I'll be who I am and I'm not a nephew of Uncle Sam
Like I said I am who I am and strong enough to get out of any jam
Jesus fed people with fish over ham
And I live from that same creed
Just add this poem to the goodness of my deeds

State farm

I come from out of space
I never been to this place
My door to life was my mother's womb
I was born in the middle of the month before June
I be holding the pen the same way the sky be holding the moon
I'm trying to expose my gift so I can feed my child with a golden spoon
I'm thinking about the future knowing it'll be here soon
I'll write as long as my heartbeat carries a tune
I'll be alright as long as I feed myself the truth
I'm as natural as the sky being blue
I'm like a dictionary so you can look at me and see words too
My image defines everything you see when the pen stop moving
My emotions never stop moving so every so often what I'm doing now
start brewing
If I don't stay true to how I feel then it'll feel like I'm losing
All I ever wanted to do is succeed beyond any circumstances
I mean what's wrong with a man trying to advance?
All this knowledge came from moments when I was in a trance
Success comes after you have belief inside your plan
And I been believing in my hand for a while
I been believing since I was a child
I know in my heart the seeds I've planted will allow me to smile

Untitled

Heaven awaits me
Time race me
Love chases me
Devil hates me
God made me
Nothing can fade me
I'm present like the sea
Thoughts ripple around me
Life won't drown me
I'm swinging every day of the week
Every hour of the day, every minute of the night
Sometimes you have to sacrifice
God give me advice
Impossible not to see me, I'm light
Impossible to grade me, I'm right
Quiet as kept, I'm a prophet with insight
God said ignore them all and just write
I'm like, you right
Now you know why I write and why I won't stop
Moving the pen be therapy for my heart
Sins of the world is off the charts
I stay in my lane as I paint my art
What you think about it?
Never mind you can't judge my talent
Even if you've never thought about it, love isn't silent
It's the loudest sound you ever heard if you were listening
And it's as colorful as the leaves on the trees during fall season
Every time I write I can hear God breathing
Talk to me lord, I have many reasons

Goldmine

Don't look past me I'm right in your face
Climbing north on the ladder at my own pace
Why do we have more than one religion for one human race?
Answer can't be found, please turn the page
I'm full of joy, but yet full of rage
Peace will come if they ever let my brothers out the cage
Spot light chasing me because I was I born on stage
I control the curtain, but I don't control the days
My knowledge running beyond my ways
I'm old fashion inside this new age
I live off wisdom, passion, and strong faith
I'm a product of what God made
Born to face the world, I'm not afraid
I'm adventurous as an escapade
The devil don't have enough water to rain on my parade
I let the love inside me arrange my pain
Nonsense inflames my brain
I'm so brilliant that the definition become strange
All I have is what I've became
I have nothing to lose and everything to gain
I got enough skills to play effectively in the game
One shot in the dark brought light to my name
Chasing your dream can bring sense to days you felt strange
I'm doing what I feel, no need to explain
I'm just putting messages in bottles hoping they find someone who had
thoughts similar to mines
My poetry will glimmer through time
Thoughts are stronger than the dime
I don't need a bank, I'm rich in mind

Untitled

Look up to the stars to see what's inside me
Heart racing at an unknown speed
I'm chasing dreams when I write and read
Glory goes to God for letting me to breathe
Free spirit, born to lead
I'm my own man, you can't model me
It's even hard to follow me
The path I take be narrow and deep
Thoughts shake me, but I'm not weak
And I'm different compared to how most be
I fear the Lord, not the police
My actions reflect the words I speak
I put my perception across these sheets
I'm deserving of who I'll become in time
Yes, my life do rhymes so don't find it hard to believe
And blessings from God I do receive
My art is my heart wearing short sleeves
You know, enjoying the weather when each moment feel special and
then you see life on a different level
What's better than life?
Never mind, nothing else is better
It's all we know and that's why most of us fear death
I'm just living and growing without skipping steps
You can't live without asking God for help
Trust me I know, without him you'll find yourself inside a dark room
trying to figure out which way to go
Well I have my light on so I place him first before I step out the door

Praying for Myself

You never heard this
Thoughts be hard as my fist
I pray for my needs
And place my wants on a list
Find me in the ocean
Last name same as a fish
I'm aiming where I can't miss
I must invest in my own gift to unwrap words I speak from my lips that
you didn't get a chance to hear but was and always will be spoken out of
love instead of fear
The truth be pure as my tears
Child of the Lord but yet they call me weird
I'm living inside the same dream I've been drawing for years and I can't
wait to go outside, but sometimes I step out to check the weather
And it be feeling good as the mood of my spirit which allow my heart to
feel like a feather
Each morning I wake up I feel different, but yet better from knowing
my eyes opened again on God's schedule
I'll be a fool not to be grateful
Love lives inside my soul so it's impossible for me to be hateful
I just follow my heart before I do what they do
I stay true to God and I, like the days do
Ignore my age because my knowledge can raise you
Until then I'll be praising the Lord because my prayers always come true!

Let it Shine

I crushed opportunities with kindness
I live without being blinded
I'm lost without finding, but yet still in traffic
I'm building a career out of what some thought to be a habit
I'm so gifted I should name my son Magic but I'm not a magician
I'm just set in my own truth like a religion
Vision full of precision
God help me make decisions and without him I revisit steps taken before
If I don't think about success I'll never see it at the door
I'm chasing things I never seen before
Only one life to live, well right now that's all I know
Positive actions is what I try to show
I'm not perfect, but I'm trying to make the distance to it close
I do what I love to do the most
When I be moving the pen time be froze
I wake up every morning because Jesus rose
Now tell me what do you have to say?
My poetry is another form of how I pray
All I want is joy in the day and peace in the night
Judge me all you want, but remember this is my life
Poet by nature is the reason why I write
Eye site has God's favor, Lord show me the light
Instead that's what I am every second of my life

From God

My state of mind out of state
Words fall every other day
For this moment now I pray
Lord keeps me under your grace
I'm black, but I love every race
Facts are taken and put in place
I open the blinds and the sun was in my face
Pictures I draw be hard to trace
I hope these moments get me through Heaven's gate
The truth isn't something you can debate
The sky wasn't something man could create
I write how I feel so my success won't be a mistake
The look in my eye tell you I'm not fake
I'm your lost brother if you can relate
Love is my father and my mother name is faith
Having one is ok, but having both is great
Wisdom is the main ingredient in the food on my plate
My thoughts need nourishment every single day
And every single night I need to pray
Before I do anything prayer is the first step I take
I know that exercise will always keep me in shape
God made me so now I'm looking for things to make
I feel like superman without the cape
You see me without knowing how much I have stored away
I'm a gift to the world, unwrap my face

"Word Up"

I hope you feel where I'm coming from as if I was grabbing your arm
I'm trying to get your attention like the sound of an alarm
Hold your breath if you need a reason to be thankful
Angels be around me when I write so I'm famous
I'm deeper than things that bother me
I'll figure it out soon enough with patience being a key
I question everything that don't make sense to me
You can't blame me because I was born to be the result of where I aimed
my dream
Knowledge is supreme and I'm similar to a dean
Wisdom has my actions clean
I'm connected to God without the sound of a ring
Do you hear me or am I being unheard
It don't really matter because that's not what I'm thinking about when I
write my words
No sweat, I'm real enough to be heard
Emotions deep, I pull them out of the pit of my stomach with nerves
The Bible say the meek shall inherit the earth so this my world
And I'm priceless versus any diamond or pearl
One day I hope to be a proud father of a boy or girl
Grateful to have either one and God know my heart as well
Maybe I'll have both to experience a different world
Until then I'm living strong, just ask each word

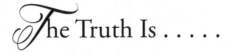

The Truth Is . . . . .

Sweet water comes from earth
Beauty is the process of birth
Living life without God hurt
Everyday my mind be at work
I wear wisdom like a pair of pants or a shirt
My rhymes is the opposite of dirt
Nobody know what goes on inside this head of mines
My poetry is not a clock, but yet it still tell time
Like the sun, I was born to shine
I'll win from how I keep trying
I'm wise enough to know peace mines
All I have to do is inhale and exhale as I close my eyes
Open my eyes and visualize everything I want and more
Spirit of a God, mind of a genius, how can I be poor?
Expect the best of me because standards of what I see isn't enough
I can't give up, my skills greater than luck
Nobody want to be smart, everybody rather be tough
Now what's up?
Where did yesterday go?
Some say it's still around, but in the form of a ghost
So tell me who really know?
At the end of the day I'm just trying to grow
Every time I opened my heart it's like looking out of a window at places
I'll like to go
And I'll get there as long as I let my words flow
I'll address each day with faith, love, and hope
I follow my own lead because God always close

Fireplace

I have knowledge of pharaoh
Born to shine because my soul glow
Thoughts move fast and real slow
Poetry is all I know
God hug me when the wind blow
I came from a sack of water that broke
They didn't tell what I should know, but only what they knew
I surpass what was told only to find more clues
These people judge me like I'm breaking rules
Life is lessons and I'm just going to school
They measure everything by pass or fail and win or lose
Competition don't exist, but expressions do
I can't ignore how I feel
I'll rather just be
My knowledge deserve more than a degree
I have wisdom all under my feet
I'm standing strong and stepping on what's weak
Even if I die, you can see me on sheets
I'll show you how I place my heartbeat on repeat
Love too deep to delete
I won't surrender or retreat
I won't stop until I feel complete
Knowing is half the battle so no reason to cheat
I'm just looking for opportunities to beat
Thoughts be open and discreet
I'm a motivational teacher inside my own speech
You can have the drama, I want peace
Its winter, but this poem was heat

Born 2 Be

They say most writers have issues so I wonder what's mine
I do feel as if I'm lost in time
I wonder if you can find me
I be jumping in and out my dream
I fly from how God blow my wings
I'm a free soul inside any scene
I'll wash this dirty world with what's clean
I do it every time I love, make peace, and pray on my knees
If you surprised from how I feel well, don't be
Just rub yourself with it so you can feel me
I'm the reincarnation of Alex Haley
Don't judge what I say
I'm just having fun baby
I was born to express myself daily
My knowledge is beyond the level of you being able to grade it
Any wisdom I obtain, I save it
And try to use it whenever I'm losing a grip
I have to stay focus, I can't slip
I came too far for my outcome to be a myth
I'm a legend at what I do, "No shit!"
Lord knows I'm grateful for what I have and get
I must chase it all
I have no time to regret
Once they figure me out, I'll be a threat
Then it'll be too late to disconnect my effect
My poems are calculated like chess
Every morning I wake up, I'll be like boy you blessed!
And for God, I'll show it
Two things won't change, his love and me being a poet

Supernatural

I write these poems and put them away
Everything has a time and place
Every step is calculated
Outcome will be how I made it
Yes it's true I'm in God's favor
Now search for reasons to hate me
I'll give to you straight, no maybe's
Poor people talk to God daily
Where would we be without slavery?
I'll do some things different but I'm still thankful for how my parents
raised me
I have a lot of manners, but I'm kind of crazy
It's hard to fill me out, you can't shade me
I'm still cool though and never shady
Thoughts irregular slashed amazing
God raising something far and beyond
I wake up each day feeling taller, I'm his son
The way I step on my times of sadness be so fun
The devil thought he had me, but I won
You can't catch me, too many words to out run
I'm running by myself, but I'm not alone
I be sitting around with thoughts all over my dome
I'm not famous, but to me I'm known
Deepest lesson learned in life, hold your own
And every day I'm trying to be strong
I'm going to sneak up on these people like a quiet storm
Let nature take its course, don't be alarmed

Study Hall

Why stop now when I have so much more to see?
After all I have faith in God and faith in me
Too much excitement around to fall asleep
Daylight is something my shadow love to see
Fear don't exist, it's make believe
God's love is all I need
If life was a book, it'll be all I read
I just want a chance to hold my own seed
In the mean time I'll complete some of the blue prints to how I'll
succeed
Learning is eternal, 360 degrees
Find out what season it is and dress for it please
The truth is hidden under all of what you see
So I'm looking to find, I'm looking to be
I didn't finish college, but my knowledge still allow me to feel free
I know how to walk across the sky and run across the seas
I do it in my mind, all from a thought I had when I was thinking
And I do that nonstop with me being surrounded by words that keep me
from blinking off my future
I must stay focus and feed insight to my pupils
I grew from my past as I witness the present and when I go to sleep I'll
see the future
Then I wake up in it because my thoughts are never stay in neutral
They move forward like the technology of a computer
When I need help I look in the mirror and ask my tutor!

Untitled

I see them watching in disbelief
Years past, but I'm still writing on these sheets
I'm still striving because my dream incomplete
I'm still riding off my inner speech
I'm still shining of my own heat
Heartbeat still dancing on beat
Future still being seen in my sleep
I wake up adding to what I saw
I'm searching for what God has for me
I'm just being myself, don't judge how I am
I'm already on the edge so I don't need anybody nudging me
Glory go to God who be hugging me like a lost child
It's funny how pain started making me smile
I'm obtaining peace as I run down hostile miles
I'm learning how to stand strong during partial trials
From it, I keep adding poems to the pile
Even when they don't listen, they still hear me loud
They judge me from their assumptions, they don't hear me out
How can you down a man who trying to accomplish what he thinks
about?
Wish Granny was living so she could read what I wrote down
I can hear her saying "Boy I'm so proud!"
That thought can make any man feel like a special child
Lord knows I'm just a special child
He didn't have to tell me to figure it out
I'm just trying to step on the stage before the lights go out
I am who I am and this is what I'm about

U Believe

My pen run laps on sheets of paper
I'm a poet who is a freak of nature
Believe what you want, but in my mind I'm major
The world be bitter until I dispense my flavor
I'll rather write what I see before I see myself being apart of how they
slave us
I try to deal with the ones I can only trust, but that idea is unfaithful
They say don't believe what you see on T.V. but every day I step outside
I'm watching cable
I dodge x-rated scenes hoping the future will show I was doing myself a
favor
You can compare me to a razor because I'm sharp and useful
Talk to me with your mouth and eyes because I'm truthful
Words so heavy it'll be impossible to move them
Thoughts pound my brain so my mind full of bruises
Measure my talent and it'll be where the moon is
Knock before you judge me because I'm inside thanking God for all
these ideas
Heartbeat regularly, like Jesus I'm real
We related by love if you read what I wrote and it give you some to feel
Emotions is a like a fruit you better peel to taste and see if life bitter or
sweet
Writing brings me joy and I always place the truth underneath
During any moments of chaos, I'll write for peace
I have many letters of love just waiting to be release
Like a caged bird flying across the peaceful sky chasing levels he never
seen
The outcome is beautiful, become your DREAM!

CHIEVABLE

How can I keep up?
Everyday thoughts speed up
I wake up in the morning feeling like I'm in a rush
I'm holding on to ideas wondering which one I can trust to take me
where I'm trying to go
Where you trying to go?
I'm trying to reach an achievable place where it don't snow over my
emotions
Instead, the sun shine over oceans and the wind I feel allows my heart to
beat in motion
My thought pattern keep sailing and my pen keep coasting across my
vision, now I'm hoping I win off my decisions
I can't run in circles as time past because that'll make me dizzy and hard
to find the outcome of me wishing one day my dream will be done in a
greater way than I previously thought
Lord knows I'm strong because he's my body builder
How can I become sick with me knowing he's my body healer?
If I don't like the cards dealt to me then I'll pray about it and become the
dealer
I don't gamble on what's not real, I scramble words around to make the
motion picture still
I'm not sick in the head, but yet very ill
I'm a heavy dose and my volume is too great to be placed inside a pill
I have the type of words that'll make the fastest child yield because life
changes around every corner
I'm a guide to it all, I wrote out my persona
You see you have to learn how to crawl through the jungle so you'll know
how to walk through the forest
My mind became rich from thinking I was the poorest
I'm more than less of what joy is
I will achieve what I conceive from my skill!

Here I Am

I have thoughts at the top of my head
I got ground under my feet
I take steps daily and sometimes I leap through life wondering what's
wrong or right
Trying to figure out if I need to go left or right
I feel like time just moving and I'm trailing it with my sight
It don't matter if its day or night
It don't matter what the surface is, as long as I can write how I feel
because life won't be still
I'm writing like I got chills from being locked inside a freezer that don't
exist
More than a gorilla in the mist, I am somebody promising
I just need to find out what dynasty I'm in because I was born a King
I see people living the American dream while I'm trying to flourish
inside my own dream
I must be misunderstood because everybody don't know what I mean
And that's quite alright as long as I make sense when I listen to me
Some call me odd because I'm like capturing moments being free
I get tired of watching what evil acts bring
Only if I could ignore it all and listen to my soul sing
Maybe I could if I sit in a room alone and pick out a poem to read
If I'm lost then this is where you can find me

So Much 2 Say

Able to touch the sky if I reach
Mind full of knowledge I can teach
Listen clear God comes out when I speak
My life looks like my heartbeat
Up and down I go on these streets
Time to be strong not weak
Time to confess not weep
Time to dig, pain buried too deep
Time to win, I don't know defeat
Wake up to anybody who's sleeping
I must fight back, can't be a sheep
I must write facts over these sheets
Dream demanding more out of me
I spell out everything, but I'm not a spelling bee
I'm showing what God did for me to feel complete
It's a cold world until you exercise your heat
I'm burning with passion until I add fire to a tree
Peaceful as the word Islam even though I don't know what religion to be
long
So am I wrong?
Before you answer I'll rather see my answer from the outcome
Too smart to ever be dumb
Too grateful not to enjoy a crumb
I'm dangerous, but don't be alarm
I don't mean in a negative way, but with a charm that's undeniable
I trust in God because he's reliable
My stubborn ways might come from my zodiac sign being a bull
It don't matter how far I travel, my love tank on full
I'm black as the man who had hair of wool

Here I Stand

Wicked days, gloomy nights
Cold ways hot fights
Love present and out of sight
Conscience ticking so I write
Nature is beautiful so I like
Every time the sun come up it be bright
Left and right isn't the only way the wind blow
So much wisdom left to learn even though wisdom is who I am
Life time shine, each hour I glow
Peace of mind needed inside a world where violence grows
Watch your steps because you could sink in the sand
Thoughts and actions go hand and hand and when it become physical
you'll see me praying
Spiritual being when it come to God I don't be playing
The Lord heard my cry "You know what I'm saying?"
Then he dried my eyes and I'm still a man
I'll conquer what I perceive and pray for what I don't understand
Born to be a winner so here I stand

My Prayer

Lord I'm learning so much through these steps I take
They judge me in the morning and when it's late
I'm standing in the middle of it all wishing these people give me a break
I learn from my good deeds and mistakes
I write to emancipate and relate to other ways
My talent runs up and down and around all my days
I'm just trying to be who I am as I walk through this infamous maze
The stories I tell be true as the words I write on each page
I live day to day hoping my love stand out over my rage
I'm standing on the side of the stage wondering if I should be on stage
I look at my thoughts to be angels helping me along this escapade
It's sad how we went from being Kings and Queens to being slaves
And what's sadder is the amount of the ones not knowing the effect it
has on today
Each morning should begin with let us pray and before we go to sleep
we need to pray
Real is when your actions matches what you say
I'm not perfect I'm still trying to improve myself
I can't do it without asking God for help
So I'm asking God for help
And help shall come, along with thy Kingdom and it will be done, just
wait, Amen!

Patiently Waiting

Time won't stop moving
Thoughts won't stop ruling
Voices inside my head asked who you fooling?
Even if I could ignore it all
What would I be proving?
I'm still breathing and far from losing
God's grace still covers me without me choosing
So I know how to love from knowing that love
Indecisive like a quarterback being rushed
I'm trying to throw a pass that I'm only willing to catch
I'm learning if I don't toss how I feel then I'll be learning how to live
with regret
Never the less, I be writing in place of my eyes becoming wet
I live off thinking the answer to my wishes is yes
Big dreams to be shared with the world when I confess
These poems be having me feeling my best
These storms be having me studying for life like a test
Tonight I hope God allow me to sleep without stress
If I'm blessed to wake up I know his love will be on me before I get dress
That's my bullet proof vest for when devils shoot mess
They mad because when I go to God's house I'm always more than a
guest
I'll be home like knowing it's a place for me to rest
God know your heart so he know I'm hoping these words bring me joy,
peace and success

ift Wrap

All I do is think,
all I do is write
I hope the amount of pain I feel shrink as I live this beautiful life,
even when unbeautiful things is happening to me
I know God, so I'm free to change any situation to my favor
All God do is grant favors
I'm not blind to what he gave us
I think love is deeper than what anybody said it was
I wonder why most people judge a person before they love
Do we blame it on absent examples of it or times being tough?
I think we all wear blame from not doing it enough
I hope people feel me from how I let my emotions and paper touch
I'm doing what I love so never will I be doing it too much
I acknowledge God when I'm walking fine and when I need a crutch
My art is the same as the picture drawn using a paint a brush
I need a museum to hang up my emotions being in a rush
I wear these poems on my face like a woman wearing blush
I got my face made up, but not with make up
It's from joy I feel every time I wake up
It's a new day, I'm entering another phase
I'm doing things my way which mean I created my own stage
My gift is affordable to all because it's open on each page

Live and Learn

I'm walking inside a world that's extremely cold
I'm a young man but yet so extremely old
I dress my thoughts in knowledge which make me extremely bold
Living is like school house I attend daily to study my soul
Giving is better than receiving was what I was told
The more I live the more I see why that was said
I'm just a strange man plus a million thoughts in my head
I'm trying my best to count them before I visit the word dead
It don't matter because God's love fill me up like bread
Eyes must stay wide on this journey so I can focus on how to make up
my bed
Courageous like David which allow me to live unlike Simon said
The principals I live off of are different than the one during school days
Sometimes life could be so scary that it'll make you afraid to face what
tomorrow holds
I'm trying to touch tomorrow from how today goes just to see if I can
carry the load
Too much traffic in your life can keep you off the road you need to be
on for success
I write from experiences in case you label it a bunch of mess
Not only I'm I a poet, but I'm the best at what I do because I can't find a
category for it to rest
Blessed be the man who keep his faith in God and in return God will be
his point of interest
Like I said I write from experience as I aim to pass the test
God is a wish provider and the answer always yes
Just follow his lead or else walk in stress

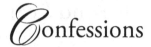onfessions

I feel like a champion
I can fly like an eagle
I'm related to people from thoughts I have
Moving a pen up and down has me perfecting my craft
I write with a frown and afterwards I'll laugh
I stay in deep thought and sometimes I visit the past
My future looking bright every time I look inside the glass
I'm vivid as the outcome and far from last
Competition don't exist, but yet I want to win so bad
I'm lost beyond recognition, but I won't give up Dad
I'm tired of this roller coaster, my stomach keep feeling upset
I know my emotions would change if I saw an ocean behind some sand
At the end of the day I'm just a simple man
I'm free as I want to be as I used my nimble mind
I grew from a seed now I see my poems growing like a vine
I write, read, think and shine
Enough vision to add sight to someone who's blind
My presence is like a window of sunlight and I refuse to close the blinds
Belief in God allowed me to draw my life in rhymes
I'm just trying to achieve without somebody judging my time
It's a bright day after every dark night so everything will be fine
I feel like I need to be myself in order to receive what's mine
Can't help but to get rich, my brain is a gold mind
Living is beautiful when you do it being kind
Search for the truth, but always know God is Divine!

Ask and You Shall Receive

I'm miles and miles away thinking about today
Aiming at any time for me to pray
Don't know where I'm headed from things I say, but I'm here to say
I'm not worried about my evolving place as long as I concentrate on
keeping a smile on my face and saying my grace before I eat
Saying a prayer before I go to sleep hoping I'm inside God's plan to wake
up in the morning
Some think I'm far out, but I'm far in
I'm trying to see joy when my scars end
Holding on to God because my patience wearing thin
I closed my eyes and gathered myself to think again
Then I opened my eyes and grab a pen
Lord, where do I begin?
Then I'll get a sense to write feeling from wondering how it feels to win
You can find me deep as my soul under my skin
Ideas of mine hard to see because I'm hanging with my angel under her
wing
I'm trying to stay warm from this world being cold during the winter,
fall, and spring
I'm sitting around wondering how long will this season lasted
Reason being, I hope the future don't be cold as the past
I get my knowledge from somebody older than the past
I'm speaking on my Lord who made me a poet when I was a seed
planted in some grass
Now everything else is how it has to be
I'm half and my poetry is half of me
Read a line if you want a piece
Until then, PEACE!

ternal

Listen out for me I'm similar to the Liberty bell
Ringing out thoughts that sometimes keep me in a spell
I'm hoping I can release myself while I'm hanging by a well
Fetching for some water because today it's for sale
People praise the dollar so much I think I'm in hell
I'm surrounded by wicked days, but I never spent a night in jail
I fight, I yell from my own emotions
Living isn't always easy so I use prayer to keep me focus
I'm still trying to figure out how tales from my mind leave me hoping
I guess its motivation to make sure my spirit won't be moping
My job is undone because its always something to do
My heart be telling me I won during any moment of truth
I'm all by myself, but my thoughts stand out like a crew
I'm young but my wisdom old as the recipe for your grandmother's stew
I write these poems for me, but yet they talk to you
Where would I be without a pen and a sheet a paper?
I guess some were looking for a clue, but instead I'm still drawing
pictures from thoughts wearing the title new
My words dangerous like karate because they kick like kung fu
I suggest you step back and slowly read what I drew because when you do
I'll be drawing again, slowly but surely I'll be clawing to a win
I might as well be compared to water because I have no end

Untitled

Eyes on the Prize
All I do is write poems
All I see is thunder storms
Chills caress my mind
I'm trying to stay warm
I'm ahead of my time, don't be alarm
Built to ignore nonsense and plant seeds inside my farm
Couple years from now I'll have trees standing behind the song the birds
sing in the morning
I'm far out because nothing I write about is boring
I'm a piece of the sky since I was brought here by the Lord's wind
I carry two swords, my tongue and pen
This may sound funny but words make me feel born again
I be thinking about the past realizing some of these thoughts was worn
then
I need to change my mind before my hair grow thin
Poet for real, been this way since I was a kid
I'll never sale my soul the devil won't get one bid
I'm wishing for peace if I was ever given one wish
Last name Bass because I swim inside my thoughts like a fish
And I'm thankful to have a father to hug and a mother to kiss
I stay lost so I use my poems as a GPS
I'm just a beautiful man who often feels pissed
Pray for me, I always can use a lift
The only job I'll like to have is writing poems during any shift
I'm a professor with knowledge flowing off my lips
Confessing to the world I am how I live
Paradise on my mind, follow me up the hill

Wonderland

I won't stop, I'll just try
I'll just live, I won't die
Look up high, stars shining in the sky
I run with the river and like the wind I fly through my own imagination
as I escape their reality
Heaven on my mind and I'm wondering if that's a place where I'll be
Right there sitting behind Jesus seat
I don't want nobody asking him who is he?
I was born to provide, saw my father do it inside my family
All I have to do first is learn how to handle me
I get answers through experience and use my eye sight as a key to open
doors I wasn't sure I'll see
Opportunity knocked so hard that it had my house trembling
Whatever I do I'll make sure I'll be in the center of things
This world have me trying to stop what winter bring
My voltage high as me not knowing the capacity of my energy
Ask me where these words come from and I'll tell you the inner me
Take your time before you read because you're about to enter ME!

Living Authority

Day dreaming brought the real day
Controlled moments taught patience
An older person can learn from a baby
It's not what I'll do after I make it
It's what I'll make from making it
I hope I bring a new way of thinking
All I know is I be writing these thoughts as much as my eyes blinking
Misunderstood what I said?
Well, I unwraps my gift frequently from sincere emotions known as
sympathy
Never will I be alone because God always near me
I grow daily and progress yearly, but some don't hear me
It's like feeling like you won, but yet asking the crowd where the cheers at?
No reply, I look away to underneath of what I see
Change come with time is some I learned from my own sheets
God said ask him and you'll receive
Faith will allow you to conquer what you believe
I write from experience and not just to be
Let these words remind you that air we use from God is free like how
love use to be, now it's some hard to see
I still think its present as a barn full of hay and I'm trying to find a key
that fell off my key chain
Look close and you'll find how I learned to express pain without causing
nobody pain
I do this to feel free or else it'll feel like my ankles and wrist in chains
And those times are no longer a picture in a frame
I was built to change rules so you can know God rule!

Don't Sweat It

Life seem like a race that never ends
How can I respond correctly if I didn't have knowledge this experience
was about to begin?
I'm not always right and I didn't have every example from men
I learned with time and I didn't always win the point I was trying to
show
I'm still trying to figure out things I don't even know
Only if I could stop the way confusing things grow
Assumptions come fast, understanding comes slow
Directions all around me, but which way do I go?
I know, down on my knees, hands together, eyes closed!
Lord protect me from this cold world aiming for my heart to be froze
I won't accept it, my thoughts too bold
Heartbeat too steady, I thanked God it don't skip notes
If I cry a river, will I still need a boat?
Who knows these things?
I'll just let the pen show how I plan not to choke
I'll just let the wind cover me like a coat
Nature has my back after the smoke clear
No fear I have, coast clear
Smile before you wear frown everyday during each year
Waste no time to show love with or without a cheer
Move forward, don't settle for the rear
Joy comes in the morning and tonight it'll still be here
Just don't sweat it, let God have it
And your days will be filled with love, not havoc

Know

You won't see the results of praying until you do it
You won't see your dream until you pursue it
Thoughts run when I don't
They move like fluid
All this pain I have
I must lose it
The future shall show how I grew from being foolish
I fixed on me with a tool known as a pen and I often use it
Never could I abuse it
I write to make everything right
So much fire inside me you can ask me for a light,
a way to learn, not the one that burn
Any and every achievement of my life I shall earn
Patience teaching me how I make it my turn
I'm not over anxious, just real concern about the answers to the question
why?
Or I'm I over analyzing things I see from my eye?
I guess I'm waiting on the moment I can tell problems bye
It don't matter who cooked it, I need a piece of the pie
This humble guy can't always be denied
I operate off my pride as I write my replies to questions of self
So much to learn inside this time I'm using my breath
I write what I feel
I write for help
I write what's real
I write what's not even there
Belief in my imagination makes me look at the reality of it with a
modest stare
Different from many, I'm so rare
Even when I'm feeling flat,
I use my poetry for the spare to keep me flowing
Faith in God keeps me glowing
Stay tune to what I'll keep on showing
Words of mind from me searching to knowing I'm real because God is!!

Perfect Match

Love God, live life
What's hard when using an applied mind?
I see no problems, just accomplishments in time
Rewind my imagination and you'll see a gray haired man holding a
feather tip pen while exposing ways to begin life all over after so much
pain been held within
I'm just discussing myself with myself hoping you can pull some from it
after you read me over again
Time blow like the wind so you must learn how to enjoy the breeze
I'm deeper than the seas when I unfold how I function
Emotions buried deep, I can feel them in my stomach
I'm writing to stay at ease and to remind myself how much more I need
to pray on my knees
I'm willing to listen so talk to me please before I lose focus of things I see
Like a little boy raising his arm to hold his father hand symbolizes my
faith as God and I walk through the scenes of these days of time
Waking up each morning hoping today I shine like that star in the sky
during the day that'll make you close your eyes if you try to stare at it
If poetry was a drug then I'm an addict, but it's much more positive
I have thoughts stored in the attic
Please don't go up there, it's too much traffic
I got letters all over the place so read why I got them
Don't judge, just witness how they'll match the outcome

Keep On Still

Life keep changing
Soul keep draining
Words still hanging
Dream still aiming
Vision keep raining
Expressions keep ranging
Talent still flaming
People still blaming
Hand keeps racing
Ink keep wasting
Thoughts still pacing
Chef still baking
Ideas keep shaking
Fear keeps breaking
Chances still taken
Love still ageless
Birds keep flying
Emotions keep riding
Pride still driving
Time still surviving
I keep striving
Heart keeps beating
Politicians still cheating
Jesus still teaching
I keep reaching
God keep seeking
The devil still hating
I'm still maintaining
Love keep falling
I keep evolving
I'm still a Poet
I still show it

Untitled

These words so loud, they don't need any music
The paper was too plain so I grabbed a pen to bruise it
You can't tell me which path to take, I'll choose it
I been knocked so much I'm still asking who is it?
No response, but it's still left up to me to fix it
I hope I'm not being too deep where you'll miss me
I can't help it, thoughts swim like fishes
I wake up every morning chasing last night wishes
I'm clean, not dirty like dishes
I can stand the heat since I was born in the kitchen
I came out the oven kicking at winning, thinking to myself life has begun
Aiming for a day to say I won!
Work load too steady to be done
Each poem makes me feel like I just begun
I don't see a limit reachable, I'll just keep growing
God's goodness still showing
Miracles happen when the wind blowing
Ask God for answers he be knowing
I'm just a student waiting for the war to end
Time heal everything just ask my pen
I was down and out when most of my peers were up and in
I'm not trying to keep up, I just want to win
I want to learn how I suppose to be so I won't think to sin
I want my blinks to grin when I look at the sky
Let my jinx end from how I comply
Passion all over the place, look at me fly
Outcome still coming, words don't die

Smile

Words all over the place like the way water be around everything
Life is a precious thing and God's goodness will make you sing
I write off my experiences and what I seen along with trying to explain
what I mean
I'm misunderstood dramatically and unconsciously, but this I'm
conscious of
Living got me falling in love over how life suppose to be
So much strange activity take place all I know is me
And all I know is him and all they see is heat coming from what I've
filmed
I write like exercises being done inside a gym
Take me seriously because I'm so serious
I be feeling like I deserve an A, but instead I'm given a B+
Which would lead to a question like am I good enough without
knowing who doing the grading
Like it's hard picking friends because some prospects will also be hateful
Everyday an earthquake take place from how the system of things be
shaking
Hold your ground while your heart keep chasing the sound
I been down so long I got good at being down
I been frowning so long so I learned how to draw a smile
I been searching so long I started jogging miles
They said God's distance was too long so I dialed
Little did I know he'll answer saying "Hello my child?"
I asked, "Where you been?"
He stated right here waiting for you to dial and that I did
Now I became found from being a lost child
I'm trying to live off my words knowing everything I wrote was worth
while
This story is to be continued, in the mean time, just smile!

Skyscraper

I'm living beyond time
I'm writing beyond rhymes
I'm still digging dirt off my shine
Brain still looking like a goldmine
I'm still aiming not to live blind
What's hard when God allow me to keep trying
I keep reading, these people keep buying
I refuse to sale my soul for any amount of dimes
What's wrong? Everything will be fine
I'm super strong from how I be lifting my mind
Thoughts stretch further than any finish line
Portrait still wet, image still drying
Voices still threats, witness how I'm wise
Despite what I see, I'm trying to strengthen my eyes
Vision so deep, words keep pressing rewind
Mission incomplete until I answer all my whys
I analyze every option and operate off my vibe
I pull my pride aside before I let it drive
Day in and day out, I find a way to survive
Some can't see my fight because I'm swinging so high
Some don't know I write because this is how I cry
I tell the truth through expressions before they call me a lie
I'm expressing myself, how can you deny?
I'm just testing myself, please stand by!
Even when I undress myself I' still fly
Diamond in the dirt presence has me feeling shy
Don't panic, attitude bold enough to tell that emotion bye
Take my ink away and I'll use dye
I'm influence as I write from my third eye
I live inside a world where words fly
I'll catch you later before I tell you bye
I jump from letter to letter across the sky

Keep Going

Listen to this cold story about a boy name Corey
His mother was on drugs because she thought life was boring
He didn't know who his father was because too many men was scoring
Corey felt like guidance wasn't meant for him
So he dropped out 7th grade feeling like school wasn't important
He started selling cocaine because he wanted some Jordans
Time past and his money later landed him in trouble
He caught a charge and saw a man in jail who had him thinking he was seeing double
Corey just found out he had a twin brother
Disbelief across his face from seeing it and hearing stories about his father, but he can't meet him because somebody shot him
Corey twin brother Torey said I started rebelling the day after
Hearts froze and these young men don't experience a lot of days of laughter
Two months later, a letter came telling Corey his mother passed away from an over dose
Pain come and goes, but here we go again
The only bright spot these brothers see is knowing their days inside a cell are about to end
Released 3 months apart, but they back together again with ideas to win
One can really draw and the other one can sing
One painted expressions, one painted dreams
If they could get over their past then you can get over yours
They learned how to love again so what are you waiting for?
Do what time does and move forward
Please, just don't give up, keep going
God will be with you in the darkest night and the earliest morning, please just keep going!

eel Me

Body full of cells, but I'm no battery
World full of spells, I dodge them rapidly
A lot of people married, but it's not happily
Change came with time because life isn't what it used to be
I wake up in the morning wondering who's here with me
I'm deep as the outcome please believe
Words I write be messages you should receive
I write each poem hoping that one was my masterpiece
Thoughts keep running because the devil trying to tackle me
I'm hard to capture, in my mind I'm free
I'll show love before I act how rascals be
I need God's grace inside this world of heat
I must acknowledge the one who allow my heart to beat
I'm beautiful from how my art speak
I'm not a crossing guard, but my words know how to direct whoever in
the streets
Honestly I'm just a friend you need to meet
It's don't matter if it's physical or if you reading me off the sheets
I'll be grateful for the opportunity, we all family
My poetry is scrutiny of me
My words go below deep
Some call me crazy because I'm so interesting
The same ones who press me like I don't know what wrinkles mean
The secret is I know the answer to everything I think about
It's just every time I try to accept it, it baffles me
I see myself running, but don't know how to grab me
Good thing I'm learning inside every reach
Everything will be alright is what I teach!

Untitled

Dreams still cover my eyes
Wings still hovering over the skies
God still saving lives
My poetry doesn't and won't contain lies
I write the truth of me every single time
You looking inside me on every single line
The greatest gift I've ever received was my mind
Man will let you down, God will let you shine
I look at my Lord when I look in the mirror and when I hold my head
up to the sky
I'm grateful to have air inside and outside
I inhale my attitude and exhale my pride
Talents instilled in me wasn't meant for me to hide
I have loose screws inside my head that get tight when I write
I feel like I can be somebody you read at night
Follow me slow or else let me thoughts crowd your sight
I have enough words to cover a thousand days twice
I built a train without any tools thinking how it'll circle life
I'll let strangers ride and the ones who believe in Christ
I'm color blind from knowing the only race is human, right?
And even with that, the truth still live under the sun
Love is one word so how can love not be one?
God is love so learn about your creator
Obtaining knowledge will allow a change in your behavior
You better save yourself during these wicked times because satan got
people doing favors
My mentality will be King until I return to dust

Closing Remarks

Too much going on, look around you
My poetry is similar to a ghetto child singing his way through
The only question stay on my mind is what do I need to do?
All the answers that can fit that question got me confused
Decisions all around me, which one do I choose?
All these battles I fight, which one did I lose?
I'm still going strong as I break the ones who judge me rules
I'm just fixing on myself using my own hand as the tool
Opportunity awaits me so I'm trying to be cool
I'm trying not to sweat
I'm trying to complete a promise and to others it's a bet
These people plain, but yet I'm a jet
My pain shoots me across the sky where the stars hanging at
They shining and twinkling in my eyes leaving me feeling blessed
I look toward God thinking do I have potential to be like the rest
I'm trying to remove that incomplete feeling from behind my chest
Some of these let down have me feeling less, but I build myself up when
I confess
I got my heartbeat on sheets pumping my best
This is how I respond to the angles of life resulting in a test
I won't panicked, I'll just read the thoughts I would've suggested
They shut their ear and eye to my confessions
That won't stop me from being somebody impressive
I pity the fool who stand in the way of how I live
God forgive!

Falling from the Sky

I see my future changing right before my eyes
I see the sun coming up in between the peaceful skies
I'm trying to dry the tears of the lost boy inside me who constantly cries
I seem to bump heads with the ones who placed their faith inside of lies
The only thing that ever comes easy is when I write down how I feel
inside
The language of my heart told my pain to be quiet
Joy belong to me like the news belong to channel five
My art is a plan that show how I handle mines
I believe Jesus is my brother and his sandals shine
I'm a deep brother from what I write on lines
All these dudes think they're tough, but the toughest thing is the time
The only time people are unattractive is when they have ugly thoughts
on their mind
I didn't pick a career at school during career day because a writer never
came
And back then it was hard to get angry from it because I didn't know
who to blame
I just stayed quiet and kept thinking about a world where poetry was my
name
So I decided to follow my dream to stop feeling so strange
God's love flow like water and in return my poems drop like rain

$\mathcal{L}$ove Me

Love me for me because I came from the aftermath of kisses and hugs
Love me for me because I'm somebody to love
Love me for me because I'm not who I was yesterday
Love me for me because last night I forgot to pray
Love me for me because God still love me every day
Love me for me because tonight I won't forget to pray
Love me for me because it's so many reasons why I write
Love me for me because holding a pen can add sight to my insight
Love me for me because I rather talk before I fight
Love me for me because I know everything don't always turn out right
Love me for me because I try to stand strong day and night
Love me for me because I'm just a man who love to write
Love me for me because I'm trying to follow the plan God has for my
life
Love me for me because I want two kids and a wife
Love me for me because I'm trying to succeed at whatever I choose to do
Love me for me because I love you!

Untitled

Can't sleep, heart off beat
Sweat like an ocean, I'm so deep
Mind state vivid and clearer than HD
Off feet when I write
Thoughts fly through the night
I'm bright as the sun
Love can make you fight and run . . . . away
I pray for myself and others
I'm just a son of my mother and father, but I have sisters and a brother
Tell me who tougher than a single parent woman?
Words keep jumping all around me
It's like playing scramble with your heart figuring out how every letter
came to be
Look both ways before you cross the street
Find God to feel complete
Anything else would be uncivilized
When I write I realize I'm a prize and a gift to the world
Nature is not a boy or girl
It's something far and beyond
When tomorrow comes this day will be done
Thoughts walk and run through my mind
And sit down on every single line
This is what I do to exercise
When they call me crazy they mean I'm so wise
Close your eyes to see pictures of what I wrote
Poems last forever, they don't disappear like smoke!

Untitled

Say farewell to the old me and hello to poetree
The one who allow people to love him from how he be
The one who poetry become a treat
Defeat will never face me and I'm the only one who can race me
I'm ahead of time so you can't pace me
I'm relearning knowledge I already knew so never again will they be able
to rape me
I'm covered in God's grace and the words I speak
I write day and night I don't worry about sleep
Every time I look at my book I feel joy beneath my chest
Heart driven but I'm not steering toward rest
I'm gearing up standing strong feeling blessed
No more standing in the rear, feeling alone and stressed
I'm here to show and tell the thoughts I confess
I'm trying to make progression every moment of the day
That way I can rest during certain minutes of the night
Every time I go to reach, it's a pen in sight
I grab it as if it belongs to me for me to write
I undress precious thoughts from dark to light
Everything come from an idea, wrong or right?
I use my heart as a home I sleep in ever night
I'm so faithful to who I am, that's why I continue to write

rtistic

Open up for the world to see
The clock keeps ticking as I breathe
I'm walking through the streets wondering if anybody knows me
They eyes look suspicious as if I'm someone to see
And my logic don't let me sleep
My thoughts under deep and I be up when the birds sing
Words bring calm weather my way
I'm outside watching the river move space
The picture drawn can't be traced
I came out the womb with this only face
Glory goes to God when I'm feeling below ok
Before I point a finger I rather give you an action that can be
remembered
Temptation tempting, but I won't deliver
This cold world will make you shiver if you can't exercise heat to stay
warm and out of harm of the wolves that lives within the jungle
Trust God and stay humble is the best advice I can give without living
for you because I had to find my own clues and places I wasn't told to
look
My poetry often leave me shook because I'm more than a book and
chances are more than just something to take
I hope you can relate, but if not stay tune because when I enter it'll be
hard to leave the room

King

Ice cold with a fever
I'll do it, won't leave it to beaver
My personality belong around people
Success must be a door you walk through
And my crazy self be running in and out the room
Holding desire to rap only because my words carry a tune
If I don't live out my dream then I'm headed for doom
I refuse to give up so I rather become the things I'm lacking of
This real talk, brother to sister or brother to brother
I shall learn and discover more levels of me
And I'll write more words to see
I trust God and who I suppose to be
I can't let your emotions stop me from being free
I'm just coasting along trying to keep my joy off of E
I'm full of love and full of peace
But yet I'm a Taurus, loyal until you dishonor me
When I write thunder speak and the sheet hold the heat
You might see fire when you read
I'm just burning desire along with completing a deed
I'm still wondering how far I'll grow from being a seed
Hard to be patient when thoughts keep speeding
I'm looking for street signs, but the light green
So I must do my thing which is show actions of a King!

Art Gallery

I'm a genius on my feet, king when I sleep
Soldier when I walk
Activist when I speak
Author when you reading me off these sheets
Poet from how I express myself so deep
Objectives being added to my journey, "Wow!" what a treat
God keep looking over and after me
Add these words to the chapter of who I am
I'm a master of my faith, church inside of me
I'm adding color to the picture at hand
I'm an artist
I write from my heart so from mines to yours, I hope you feel it
My poetry is a structure of me and I'm still building
And I'll never get done because learning is eternal
My words so adequate, they can be a sermon
I'm picture perfect without a camera
You won't find my way on T.V. channels
I already won so I don't consider my actions to be a gamble
I hope I motivate you to think like when you playing scramble
I be holding on without holding a handle
Words be at the top of my head like fire on a candle
And the day I see a beach I'll be wearing a pair of sandals
Consider this to be beautiful art on a canvas

Untitled

I'm standing on the edge with one foot in the air
I'm about to jump knowing God will catch me some where
I'm holding too much inside to bear
Pain can't be an outfit I choose to wear
It never felt right
I'm laced with the truth and it's sealed tight
Nobody or nothing can infiltrate what I write
It's a gift from God that allow me to appear bright
Take me where love is a common sight
This world feels more like a strange place
Don't feed into the nonsense, lose weight
I always monitor my plate
My life wasn't born from chance, it was fate
Don't judge how I walk if you don't walk this way
I must pray for myself and these nights and days
Knowledge is freedom from thinking like a slave
I follow the man in the mirror, my heart really brave
I'll just have to be the way I am
Life is not a playground so therefore I'm concern

Day Dream

Birds chirping during morning hours
The sky keep opening up like a flower
The wind is calm and the trees stand with strength
The grass is full of all kinds of insects
And the soil rich where worms at
The river still smell like summer at its best
The water glowing from the sun's glare
No clouds around just the air
Flies, bees, and butterflies keep flying under the birds
Frogs hop from one spot to the next
Turtles are moving in a slow direction
Squirrels and rabbits chasing each other for fun
Heat is being release from the sun
And the day goes on
The sky begin to fade into orange
The sunset is starting to form
Bees, butterflies, and birds go to bed
Mosquitoes come out as the owl sits in the tree looking out with eyes
spread
Then the night sets in and you can feel a breeze every thirty seconds
Such an award after hard labor or learned lessons
Nothing compares to nature
I express myself like each day on paper
And the pen fall with the night
A complete feeling is what I feel after I write

Who can tell me how great I be?
Who really know the depth of the words on the sheets?
It's what I feel and what fills me
Chasing what thrills me
A 9 to 5 isn't the greatest place to be
I'm still growing, I'm still breathing
My style can be worn during all seasons
Reasons be the reason why I write
Alone in the dark until I carved out light
Now I'm standing out shining as I leave foolishness in the past
Anxious to meet success, but yet I won't live fast
I'll just keep moving as I smoke my grass
Sit alone and laugh over the hard times
I know all about them, but won't press rewind
I just live my life according to these lines
The seed be planted when I write and actions are born when I speak my
rhymes
I'm writing from a part of me you can't see
Why question who I am when my words speak for me
I pull strength from holding on to what I believe
I feel like I'll achieve everything I think about
After all the joy God gives,
it's enough to sing about but I can't sing but then again maybe I can
I was about to end this poem,
but its starting over again like one leaf fell then the wind started blowing
again
Funny how a pen keep me far from sin
Wow, I'm having a good time with how I'm feeling within
Peace until the next time I do this again
I won, the referee holding up my hand

ose Garden

I'm sitting from afar witnessing a fight between a man and his emotions,
between knowing and his notions
So much to think about inside an era where everybody scream and shout
I'm trying to figure it out, but too many opinions standing in the way
Never will I know enough not to pray
Even when I'm feeling gloomy I have potential to shine like the sun
inside a day
Impossible to hold down such a force when it's growing in your face
Why race against fools if you know the content of your pace?
People judging as if I didn't wake up in God's grace
Funny how they placed me as if they control my fate
My poetry will meet me at Heaven's gate
No thoughts of dying just referring to how my words hold faith
Drop what in a collection plate?
I don't like the type of food they be putting on my plate
So don't ask me did I eat when I show you I haven't ate
My vision amongst the stars so how could my truth be unreal
Let me just pay attention to it like I do because you can't present
evidence for my case
I'm not guilty, but they keep putting me on trial all over the place
I might bend, but Lord knows I won't break
He built me to be this way, so in it, I'll stay
My knowledge beyond your thoughts of me so put these roses in a vase

rite

Write with a sense of urgency
Write when I feel the devil near me
Write all the fear out of me
Tears always fall with peace
I took the war out my mind so it wouldn't exist to me
Write to feel free
I do have a right to be
I shadow what follows me
Write from my heart so at some point you'll feel me
Write because the paper too plain to see
Writing is a gift for you from me
Write to uplift, write to not slip down the devil's creek
Write to show I'm in the family of the meek
Write to stay at the top of my peak
Write to show no signs of being weak
Write to allow the way I feel to leak
Write in my sleep, but the process is called dream
Write to show all what I mean
Write because my being is Supreme
Write to show my words and actions are on the same team
Write to scream
Write to sing
Write to plant seeds
Write to stay on key
Write to unlock who I truly am
Look in the mirror and write what I see
The picture getting clearer as I write
Write to show what a perfect picture look like
And I might not be perfect, but I'm perfect when I write

As We Dance

When I grab a pen I don't know how it'll end
I just write how I feel across the wind
Aiming to win because life change over and over again
God stay the same and sometimes I feel like I'm insane
Membrane above strange
Thoughts circle my brain
I can't fail at what I love to do
I can't judge you so I stay in my lane
All alone so I'm the only one to blame
I'm smoothed as the day I came
On a peaceful morning I entered the game
Taking position and holding my name
And today it's still the same
I can't get comfort from maintaining
Going beyond will feel more satisfying
Writing brings joy every time
Flow like a river, I don't force any rhymes
Not following your dream is like committing a crime
I wake up to mines when I open my eyes
I'm creating more scenes with time
Blessed be the one to keep God first and on mind
Funny how what I just said be on line
I have the floor, the pen dancing with mines

Air Fill

I'm exploring myself
Rich in mind so I'm exploring wealth
Thanking God for my health
I always hope my words offer help
I'm trying to live beyond the word death
Life all I know, I don't know nothing else
Everything they said was right seem more to the left
That's why I write how I feel in depth
Detailing what I saw hoping you see what I felt
I'm reaching for the stars the same way I take steps
No scars on me from the past just to show I was well kept
I walk in God's glory so the presence of harm isn't there
You live and learn, I go straight when others turn
My playing time became a time to learn
Come close and you'll feel the heat from a passion that continue to burn
Write from outside my head because most times I am
Love pure enough to disarm any scam
My thoughts louder than instruments used in battles of bands
I'm just a man acknowledging some of the thoughts that surround me
I keep writing because it's more to read
Poetry in me like the air we breathe

isten

I'm on rhythm with why I'm living
Heart keeps beating and I'm a witness of God's love
Judge me for what?
I'm just doing what I love
Believing in myself as my ability keep adding up
I'm just pouring out who I am because I don't belong in a cup
My thoughts pick me up like a bus and take me to a place where I don't
have to fuss
As I write down what's inside me without being in a rush
Giving is sharing and I'm reaching with my touch
I keep scorching paper waiting for the arrival of a fire truck
Flames unseen so I guess it's not burning enough
Vision clearer than ever now that I know which way up
I have to maintain how to stay on top
I don't write all the time, but my thoughts still on a clock
I'm ready to sail, tired of my ship being tied to the dock
I was built for greatness, it's only right for me to show off
I'm soft spoken, mild tempered, but my poetry not
I mean I'm always in thoughts until my heart stop but right now it's
growing
Love pouring out and I continue to write because I have a lot to think
about
These poems so good I deserve to be singled out
I'm still creating ways for you to hear me out
Have you ever heard a quiet man scream and shout?
Listen

merging

Grant me this, a place where Jesus exist in the flesh so we can talk about
this mess
Where did it all go wrong?
It's like we're strangers at home and at heart alone and scared to let go
of what's being told by others as if it's the truth without question as my
thoughts keep moving in all types of directions and I was born to show
affection and at night I don't rest and sleep, my eyes just be closed as I
continue to think knowing God control the time my eyes will blink
Now I'm back in this world looking for more clues to deliver such news
of me because I'm important the moment they stop listening and the
times before
The future is a gift that opens up like a door and I'm walking through it
showing what's true to me
Feel me? And if you don't, hey it's not my fault
This is who I am and this is how I walk, how I read and how I talk
Learning is a beautiful thing to do so thank God for knowledge and
when you exercise it, then its power
And they judge me as if they know my hour
Clueless to the fact my poetry is a flower in the summer time and a
blanket for when it's cold outside
All this love I carry comes from inside and down the river of my true
spirit where I shine
You witnessing my greatness and I can't be denied!

ordsmith

Clouds invading the sky
Stars twinkle through the night
The wind calm as my behavior
Life is such a flavor
Peaceful like a good neighbor
Love you without it being a favor
Poetry is what I savor
Doing what you feel is not labor
It's a picture without cable
Heartbroken, Cain still killing Abel
I'm your brother who's able to love
The world filled with hatred and it's corrupted
Violence isn't a characteristic of the creator
Such ways doesn't belong to us
I refuse to adopt a negative manner
I need blessings, not curses under my sandals
Thoughts swing down like a hammer
I'm just trying to fix what's broken from the camera
Change won't come until we change the channel
Or am I just a lonely candle?
Holding a flame like it's a handle
Thoughts always moving because I can't control them
Poet at heart and I write with a motive
A commander inside this art of war
Mind state started off poor
Now I have a goldmine in store
I live off words, from the Lord

On my Way

I walk with a purple heart
My thoughts cover this green earth
I'm exposing what's been in me since birth
Words quench my thirst
The last shall be first
Life is a gift without the curse
I know how to respond to a storm
Still mourning over family and friends that's gone
No reason can equal me being wrong
I express myself and move on
I plant seeds for better moments
The men in the Bible was my homies
And you don't know how many thoughts I'm at home with
I can speak without words coming off my lips
Wisdom deeper than myths
I always press the clutch before I shift
The pen always X-ray my gift
I'm super strong from all these thoughts I lift
I'm trying to add love to the world over bullets to a clip
I'm running so fast I hope I don't trip
The past is the vehicle that got us here and the ride always bumpy when
we don't let God steer
Sometimes I'm so lonely my only company is a tear
Trust the fact I'm ok, but won't settle for being in the rear
My position is to lead without fear

Reason Being

Once again attention being paid to my thoughts
Each day I find something I lost
Nothing is more beautiful than life itself
I'm just chasing precious moments I never felt
I know I've been woke more hours than I've slept
I want to be placed in a position to help
The face I see in the mirror surly will get me there
I still give respect to older men by saying "Sir!"
It's a cold world, but yet they say it's fair
I'm just trying to enjoy this air because stressful moments will take away
your hair
I'm still holding smile within me I've yet to share
It's a never ending story to the thoughts I wear
Writing will always comfort me and magnify how much I care
My art keeping sounding off like a drum of a snare
I walk with confidence and my poetry carries a glare
I'm no intruder because I was born to be here
Keep listening for me since I'll be speaking through years
Showing all how I achieved a dream through facing fears
And showing why I smile and hold tears
Beyond it all I'm standing strong with my head up
I'm a part of God's glory, this not luck!

ial Tone

What strike me to write?
The intuition of my thoughts
Precision with my vision as I discover how time is not lost when you
focus on what your heart desire
Love is my attire as I proceed to do things what some think makes
believe
I retrieve knowledge from my ancestors with speed
My blood stream holds the DNA of Kings and Queens
They can hear how my spirit sings
Everywhere I go, joy is what I bring
The cream of the crop is me
You don't have to be as confident as me, but please don't judge how I be
I live without rules and time doesn't monitor me
I'm free so don't compare me to what you heard or see
I'm different, thought pattern carry spirits
I dance to more than one type of music
Too real for a movie so your camera will catch glory
Don't look over the words from seeing the flesh of the story
I am who I am with the Lord
Rocks thrown at my fence will have you ducking from the blade of a
sword
I'm everlasting if you don't know it
I have passion and like the wind it keep blowing
They was toying with my gift, but I'll show them the deepness of my
roots
Thoughts are fruits I eat daily and I been thinking since I was a baby

Untitled

It's hard to keep up with how much I write
I do this day and night
Pictures keep deriving from my other side of vision
Words always keep people attention
And I don't have to play games to keep winning
I'm a teacher, just keep reading
I deliver what's supreme and real love is a powerful thing
The pen keep moving up and down like my chest as I breathe
I wake up aiming to succeed and go to bed swinging at what's left
incomplete
Failure just introduce a lot of more ways to think
Poetry is an introspection of me
Loving yourself is the door to being free
I keep drawing because they never seen me
I'm the main event, but yet they treat me like I belong where the screams
at
Wow, I'm what a dream is
Heart keep pumping with every reach
Born to teach, all goals will be completed
Pain is just something to delete
Love is just actions to repeat
I walk with the wind and converse with the breeze

Sorcerer

All I have is hopes and dreams
All I see is pictures of scenes
All I hear is voices and screams
All alone but yet I feel like I'm on the winning team
I fall asleep with success on my mind
I wake up feeling like I'll succeed
I keep writing on these horizontal lines exposing how my life be
I love myself even if they don't like me
I'm trying to do the right thing like Spike Lee
I visit Heaven during moments I be writing
Holding the pen makes my heart feel light
Funny how the wind can't be seen during the day or night
Now you know why life deeper than your eye site
Every since Eve took a bite of that apple people be searching for what's
wrong or right
I ignore the drama as I examine my life
Knowledge keep me free and love don't have a price
My heart light as a feather and love heavier than nice
My art is perfect weather for any day or night
That's why I write between the sun and moon
I be inside time like it's a room
People be outside judging until I reach for the broom
Then I swing it around like it's the only fan that'll keep me cool
My knowledge could be added to a curriculum at a school
In life you have to learn how to build because your thoughts are tools
God don't make mistakes so we have power not to, but do because we
have no clue
30 years before I had a clear idea of what to do
Now I know how to listen to God and dance off my heart beat
You won't find the hurdles I jump at a track meet,
but I'll show you where they located if you ever asked me

Young and Restless

Thoughts of a winner inside my head
Actions of a poet is starting to spread
No plans to stop because I'm not facing a red light
Time don't stop so why should I?
I look to make progress like a new born child
I'm anxious to learn
I'm anxious to smile over the frowns I hold inside
I guess my journey is the meaning of worth while
Since birth my dreams been accumulating in a pile
I fight during tribulations and I'm innocent in my trials
I call God and the conversation last many miles
I'm trying to take a clear shot, body numb from all the fouls
It's hard to find rest, my eyes be open like an owl
I'm too blessed to feel down so these words make me proud
Search for me in the clouds because I'm beyond what some believe
Trust in God keep me relieved and life is something to read,
but I don't know how many chapters exist
I'm just living to learn so I can watch out for what some might miss
Mother Nature hugs me daily and I kiss her back like this
I see in a genius in the mirror and the signs of it are across these sheets
Excuse me but this pen is the utensil I use to teach
My mind is not full, but I'm mindful of what's in reach
Everything I ever dreamed of, yes indeed
Tears of a soldier will be left on the battle field
I'm destroying what's fake with what's real
Now you know why I stand for and forever more
I'm just doing what I was sent here for

The river that's in me

The future can't hear the past and the present can't hear the future
My eyes are more than pupils
Every sunrise is beautiful
Every morning I wake up is a miracle
Strong evidence that God close as my tears
I'm in tune with my purest self
Rest assure my vibe is good for your health
I'm writing what's felt from how I feel
How can you hinder me from me?
I'm on a journey of peace
I peep at the future when I'm sleep
Then I wake up feeling unique
I'm counting actions that equaled the outcome
I'm inside manhood feeling cool and calm
No harm shall ever be caused by what I'm doing
I ignore the world and keep pursing a life designed for me
God see me and you can't disagree
I try to stay in his sight so demons won't grab me
I stay true to who I am and walk past them as they reach
They can't touch this is the lesson at hand
I'm such a man
I just follow my commands
And dance in the wind free from sin
Asking God to help me win,
but then I think I already won because the ink from the pen was born
So now I shall watch it grow which means forever from me words will
flow

elow Deep

Seem like I'm back on stage
Well my words back on pages
They ignore my efforts while I give it praise
I'm the beginning to a new day
That's why more and more I need to pray
The sky covers me in every way
I'm delighted by its beauty and how my words show how the picture
shape
It's like having pieces to a puzzle and each day one is laid
I'm adding color to a picture I been drawing for decades
Thoughts move like a parades because they march every day
I'm too wise to be afraid and too smart not to pray
Mindful of what I'm doing today so tomorrow I'll have my way
I don't know which way I'm headed because I'm still creating
Desire keeps the fire burning and lessons show me what to appreciate
The world keep turning, but God only knows the true date
Moving this pen display sounds of a violin as I dance with my fate
The food I serve isn't the type you put on a plate
I'm expressing how I feel because I can't cope with being a fake
Each poem is meant because God don't make mistakes
I'm great, I believe in myself when no one else can relate
Words are bond and some you can't break
I have the strength of a warrior with a King's mind state
When blessings come I be in place,
steps then be hard to trace
So I'll just move right along and the fight might be long,
but I'll still stand strong
And withstand the wind that's blowing from the storm,
but at the end the sun will show a day that's warm
I'll be enjoying the weather as if it was the reason why I was born

129

What is poetry?

Poetry is a blessing, poetry is expressions
Poetry hold lessons, poetry is aggression
Poetry is protection, Poetry is affection
Poetry is direction, what's poetry?
Poetry is deep, poetry is me
I move like poetry in these streets
Poetry is the ground holding my seed of belief
Poetry gives me relief, poetry bring peace
Poetry is what makes me feel free
Poetry gives shade like a tree
Poetry don't rain on me, poetry show how the sun speak
Poetry shining within me, poetry covers the alphabets A-Z
Poetry don't sleep, I wake up in poetry
What's poetry?
Poetry governs me, poetry let me be
Poetry allow me to dance without my feet
Poetry is my heartbeat
I'm thriving inside of poetry
Surviving because the Lord with me
Poetry is a language I speak
Do you understand my poetry?
It's the truth of me vs. everything I see
What's poetry?
It's a group of words explaining how I feel because poetry has nerves
Poetry is a diamond, but when directed toward a woman it's a pearl
Poetry has no time and poetry is the definition of my rhymes
Poetry is not a crime, poetry is mine
With poetry I'm fine
Poetry be smiling and crying
Read poetry and between the lines
Poetry is on my mind

Moving Along

A few tears fell, but nobody saw it
Dreams cover me like clothes inside my closet
Hard to stay positive when you wake up feeling heartless
No more room for stress, just room for targets
I feel like a lost boy walking between projects
Piss poor and stomach continue to hurt from me starving
If Heaven just another door then I'm still carving my key
This cold world at night makes it hard to sleep
I won't feed into the non sense so I'm just writing what's against my
conscience
Prophet at hand so devils take this as a warning
I'm just now releasing some of the things I was born with
I exercise the truth against endless myths
This is a sinful world so be careful along your trips
I chase the way I feel to keep myself apart from the made up script
I don't follow people who do the same things year after year
My beliefs keep God here and the devil over there
He be across from me looking into my eyes hoping I stare
I stay focus and remain humble as I inhale and exhale air
I'm very different and quite rare,
but my knowledge is terrific and thoughts are what I wear
I'm so thoughtful inside this jungle I can communicate with a bear
And Jesus had to be black because I have wooly hair
I never mean to offend anybody with the pen
I'm just expressing myself
Money make the world turn for some,
but for me it's the thoughts I share
I'm a diamond in the rough,
but yet I'm shining through the dirt
They say the truth hurt,
but it makes me feel good
I'm steering my dreams like an automobile with my soul being the
engine under the hood

oint Blank

I'm still moving with the Holy Spirit
I'm still writing in a way were people feel it
Wisdom so loud, I'm sure you can hear it
All is well I don't know what tears are
Until they fall from my eye, but right now I'm a star
Vision so sharp it'll leave more than a scar
Lord continue to help me like you always do
In my own personal way let me show everybody you true
Thoughts keep raining down showing many clues
Problems are temporary, I have too many tools
I'm rolling like a wheel, but I'm the inner tube
I don't aim to break them, but yet I don't follow any rules
I have redemption on my mind knowing what it'll do
Another way of life is approaching and I'm anxious for it too
I stay true to who I am hoping God give me extra credit
Even I know all these poems equal a whole lot of seconds
Teacher at heart between the lines are many lessons
I don't trust what everybody say because we all have our different
questions
Art of war at hand and my brain is the truest weapon
I'm not catholic, but yet these are my confessions
Glory goes to God because this how I make my progression
And I'm still on the journey of living without stressing
Whenever I have a child I'll be next to the closest thing to Heaven
Yea I'm spreading the word, but I'm no reverend
I'm just a child of God who receives many blessings
After dreams I keep fetching and stay in shape from how my thoughts be
stretching
So I'll drop the pen and pick it back up with the next one

ingtone

Here comes another episode, thoughts always on patrol
I can't stop I'm on a roll and the world still very cold
I'm still black and bold, state of mind nothing but gold
I'm moving along, but God in control and that's something I'm not too
proud to know
Assume nothing wait until I tell you so
I accomplish more when I let my emotions go
And I don't live fast I just breathe slow
I had to learn the fact you can't be scared to grow
You can't be afraid to know who you really are
My soul similar to the sky and my spirit is a star
I'm shining against any judgments from afar
I'm still living, the world still turning and I'm still learning things to know
Of course I'll be great at doing what I love to do the most
The clock just struck to show all this talent I been holding so close
I already know what's going to happen when I let go
A story you never knew will be told
My gift ageless, it can't become old
You'll be amaze with all the pages I have to unfold
I rather go outside than sit inside and be unknown
Pride hard to judge, but yet it gives me foundation to areas where I'm strong
I might be odd, but smart enough to tell you what's wrong
God the teacher inside the class of my own
I add color to what's already drawn
My poetry is a place where I belong
Even when I leave the house I still be at home
Peace all through my dome
Dreaming of who I can be put me in a zone
I hope these words tell you my voice will never be gone
Quiet as kept, but yet I know you hear my tone

Miracle on Westmont Street

I'm so fresh, with or without the pen I'm blessed
All praises go to God, but other than that I'm next
Respect me because I give respect
Paper become mirrors to my soul when I'm feeling stressed or upbeat
I write what I feel or else I'll feel incomplete
Life feels like a race and I'm just now approaching the lead
I'm so fresh and so clean
Art mean the chase of a dream
Success mean mission accomplished, but yet now I have more dreams
More art to paint, more scenes to face
God is ahead of my life and for that reason I'll pace my efforts
Knowing I want to become a person to help us
I understand the fight and struggle of the unjust
I'm the voice of the unheard
You want poetry well here it is as I write from a feeling that came over me
No controlling me, free spirit
Behind my skin and blood my soul is buried deep
A blessing is being able to breathe while you sleep
The only thing colder than the streets are the police
That thought don't bring peace, but let that be what your actions
produce
I'm feeling so juiced up don't know what to do
I'm exposing how I am when my thoughts and I are alone during hours
most are sleep
I'm up being me, to know God is seeing me
I'm living proof indeed
My dreams move at an unbelievable speed
I'm a scientist, give me room to think
I'm on the brink of discovering me
No holding back, I'm unfolding like the message in the bottle
Lost poet from across the ocean starving for moments to live and survive
simply off what I think
Yea that's the miracle I'm striving to be

Poetic Faith

Ignorance can't caress my mind
The air I breathed in shines so I'm glowing as we speak
Never will I be too old for eyes not to leak
Each poem you hear or read from me is a treat
Well I hope that's the way people see it to be
Poetry is what God gave to me
So I'm living through words and days I see
I know who I am, but I'm still fighting to be
I know it sound strange, but it's the truth honestly
I'm not real religious and still be blessed abundantly
Don't judge my character if you don't know the plot of the story
Lord what's wrong with these people?
They don't see that I'm caught inside your glory
I wonder how life would be without money, lies and boasting
How would the church scene change if they go beyond hoping
So much news about the aftermath of a gun barrel smoking
No leadership, no focus, just devilish promotions, but through it all I
keep going
And knowing it's a reason why I glow
Reasons why words show how I feel more and more and reasons why
knocks keep coming from my door
Opportunities keep coming from the Lord and my tongue is like a sword
cutting any evil acts pouring down on me
I'm soaring past catastrophes knowing God keep grabbing me
So it's hard turning my back on what invented me
POETRY

Laying on Sheets

Feelings tied up
Eyes closed shut
They judge but don't know what
They should be trying to hug a brother
Ask my mother, they treat me like a problem
Make me want to holler sometimes
Rewind the past and you'll see right now
Quiet as kept but I'm proud
I learned how to listen when I was a child
And exercise that during my trails
I'm in the afternoon of my life, watch the night turn wild
Inside I frown, outside I smile
Life have up's and downs
Don't get too close, I don't trust who around
I was a poet before they found out
Maybe that's why they count me out
They downing me as if they don't know how
I'm still trying to smile over these hard times
I write hard rhymes from a soft side
I can't hide from myself or lie
Honesty is what holds the sky
Loyalty is what holds my eyes
I write time after time
I am who I am line after line

To the Future I Go

I be writing these episodes to show how my thoughts explode from my
head to the paper
I'm no faker or stranger to this moment
I'm starving for success so I can't be around you if you're not hungry
My stomach be growling
I'm from a city that don't value dreams, well that's how it seem
Tired of arguing with ones who don't believe
So leave me alone, I can't accept how things are
I'm not an employee, I'm a star
They like to hang around, I like to go far
No time to explain, I hope you know I mean that's what experiences in
life show
You can either sit still or grow
Just know it's your choice or your lost or victory in sight
I write like this the first poem I'm writing
I'm still excited
Fire burning from desires of mine that's still bright
Thoughts be taking flight
Don't tell me what's wrong, tell me what's right
Don't judge me in the morning
Don't judge me at night
God read actions while you reading about Christ
I don't know what's wrong or right so I won't act as if I do
I'm just living how I see it to be in my eyes because they're lying all the
time and I don't have time for it while they keep supporting it
That's where we clash
I'm too futuristic to live in the past

My Mental, Physical Life

Running to the moon, please don't leave the room
I'm art without the canvas
My hands don't belong in handcuffs
I'm a bit much when I stand up
Don't be scared of a Giant showing love
Who said violence would come from a black dove?
Silence is what I hear when I speak up
I'm an A student, but some treat me like a C+
I'm on a journey earning my own trust
I have the type of knowledge that'll pick you up like a bus
Everybody standing still, eyes still turning moist
Even if I become hoarse, I wrote down my voice so you could hear me
clear
No place to go without God being near
He's always on my mind so I'll never be thoughtless
My life representing how God blesses
I'm not an envelope, but yet I'm always holding messages
You won't find my kind at your registry
I came out the womb alone so it's hard not to feel like I'm Heaven sent
Why question this when the answer in the midst
Life is a woman I'll love to kiss
My heart pounding like I'm facing an unstudied for test
Experience being the best teacher is an educated guess
This I know
I live my life as so

Natural Reaction

I'm writing down how I feel because my thoughts won't be still and I'm
deeper than the word real
All I'm trying to do is live and ignorance getting on my nerves
This is a cold world
Experience the best teacher even when it comes to a girl, I mean woman
or female
My poetry is a spell I been under since I entered the world
Caught up inside who I am, nothing else really interested me in the
physical realm
I'm different is a fluid I love to spill and it flows around well and it's always
there like water from a well or water around a whale
I speak on my behalf because my thoughts are hard to tell
Thank God for the fact you can still learn after you fail so tell me what could
really hold you down other than yourself
I'm proud to be me and clouds in the sky are a special treat to my eyes and
the river moves without lies so God is true and that's what nature prove time
and time again
What else can you feel without seeing like the wind?
I'm not clueless of the place I'm residing in
I take the tests of life with actions, but yet study by using a pen
I'm my own friend
I know him so I try to stay away from sin
I know you caught up in what I'm saying, but this poem has reached the end

Never Absent, but Always Present

Biblical days, unlawful ways got the world in chips like Lays
You are what you eat so I hope you don't fade away
Life is a book and I let God turn the page
Too much love inside me to live in rage
Peace follows me through each and everyday
Odd but yet super straight and too real to be fake
God is good, God is great
I prevail over any judgment and emerge past hate
Trouble don't last always, but God's love do
I'm sitting here day dreaming about my logic and how it's natural as the
sky being blue
I write myself clues as I proceed toward the unknown
I'm strong, not wrong
I'm just walking through life with thoughts drawn
I'm still critiquing the picture I've had inside my head for so long
My gift can prolong through time so hold on
I was born to shine so don't think I won't
I'm hard to be found, I'm always lost
I grabbed the pen to find paths to cross
I'm always going deep, but I'm not Randy Moss
I'm watching where I step because in some areas the ground is soft
Life is natural, but yet it still cost
This world so cold that summer time produce frost
I sit with God daily so his presence in my life isn't lost

efense

The river still flow and birds still sing around my heart
Funny how the pen hold me together when things fall apart
I won't give up because each morning is a new start
The present exist but then again it don't
And judging me is more like committing an assault
It's hard, but I'm still surviving inside of times that's lost
Words travel so I thank God for my voice
I guess being able to make a decision is a choice
I'll forever stand behind who I am with no remorse
Before I accept defeat I'll create more ways to score on the court because
I don't see an end zone
What if I told you I write when I'm alone?
Well, I guess I'm a lonely man, but hold on
I'm just looking at life through another stance
Trying to stay balance in a world that's unbalance
Violence occur more than times of peace
Lies spread more than the truth being seen
So much seem weird to me, people act like unanswered questions are
answers to believe
I'm different from most so be careful of what you give me to perceive
I be up all night writing wisdom for you to read
I been fighting so long you can't see me bleeding
Time keep rolling on and I'm still breathing
Success is within my lungs so I'm achieving when you think I'm not
Another poem wrote to prevent any stumbling block
I feel good about it so now the pen will drop

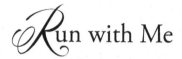# Run with Me

Things change when your actions do
Your heart beat only because God tell it to
Such a shame how some live without a clue
How can every day be the same when each day is brand new?
I cherish life as I try to be mindful of things I do
My hair short, but it's still time for me to let it down
I could tell you a lot about women and frowns
I'm living dreams searching for adventures that'll arouse me
I get bored fast as I'm often sitting somewhere deep
They say it's lonely at the top,
but I'm still climbing to see
Knowing if I closed my eyes the man in the mirror still will be looking at
me holding me accountable for goals I didn't complete,
levels I didn't reach and opportunities I had to teach
I must be strong over weak, must be woke instead of sleep
Life priceless, don't treat it cheap
I'm taking a leap toward faith and I refuse to fall between the creeks
My love is intact like the words I place on sheets
Myself is who I'm living to be
I don't follow, I lead
I don't stop, I proceed
I even plant seeds, as you can see I love to write and I also love to read
So read me because I'm an untold story to be continued because my soul
still speak through windows of obscurity
I see more than you hear from me
So I keep writing to release my consciousness to improve my common
sense because so many are unconscious and I try not to get caught up in
that nonsense
So I write, I mean I run, no I sprint

From Scratch

I'm writing through time
Life on my mind
Scenes on lines
Smoke between my eyes
Peaceful like a cup of tea before dinner time
Having the type of conversation that'll subtract crime
Love should be shown as much as you hear the sound of the word,
but that's not realistic in this world so it seem
Sometimes I want to scream, but that won't do anything
So I grabbed a pen and write how I feel the way the wind blow
Natural and on time to show how my words came to be
Raise your arms to hug instead of showing the position of how a gun
aim can be
Despite the season, nature is always something to see
That's a fact that'll never be incomplete
Like my skin being black like the ink to the words on the sheet
Grateful every moment my heart continue to beat
No surrender, no retreat, remember my art is always neat
Well that's an opinion by me until you judge me
Some hold a grudge without knowing what a grudge is
I use to do it until I found out its unhealthy
I do what I feel which is what God tell me
He's my guardian, he won't fail me
He love and respect me
He gave me free will so I choose to be drug free
I'm nothing but what the Lord made me

lessed

Wool pulled over my eyes
It's dark inside even when the sun outside
Living off pride, but that can be dangerous
Weird how a drug can be called angel dust
I'm not judging, I'm always looking for Mary to puff
I'm opened minded, what do you want to discuss?
The world full of lust, lies, and mistrust
Against the odds I have rich blood
Prevailed past moments I was stuck in mud
Knowing God is present every time my eyes open up
Funny how they'll question who I trust
Forgive them Lord, they be judging a bit much
I'm about actions, they about kissing up
Patience the best defense against times you think to rush
Slow down, hold up, I'm sure God didn't create me in a fast manner
I can be an object for a camera
My soul shine and waves like a banner
Thoughts hit hard like a hammer
Too many loose screws to handle
So just let me Be who I am inside this grammar
Unleashing knowledge that'll educate ones who locked inside the
slammer
I'm your lost brother from Heaven
My words bless me over any seven or eleven
I won't gamble what God gave me or sale it
Life precious and something to be cherished
I can't rest too much to confess so the pen keep moving toward emotions
to address
My objective is to create progress
I'm proud of myself even when holding stress
Only if I can let it go so I can fully feel blessed!

I'm Alive

Window image, thoughts are driven
No ceiling can contain me
I stand too tall
And drop words the way rain be coming down
Why frown?
Life too short, smile
Wisdom I hold come from many miles away
First pray, draw your plan then trace it in the physical world
Don't chase a girl or woman if you don't know how to make her smile
Consider that to be a free throw, don't foul
My eyes be open like an owl
And I run like the river
I write to make my vision clearer
Thoughts always pure,
born from an unseen world like a baby,
thinking is Heavenly
Hear it from me, not T.V.
You know how poetry be
Words infiltrate your heartbeat
Impossible not to feel me
I write what I feel
Sick ones I'm the one who heal
Don't sale your soul for a cheap thrill
Everything moves, even a minute can't be still
So how can I hold up for a minute?
I can't, I have to keep living

$\mathscr{A}$ Whisper Said . . . . . .

Swing with all you got despite how the pitch thrown
Knock it out the park and I don't care where it was sent from
They say opportunity only knock once so don't settle for crumbs
Too many people to feed by using your tongue
Be who you suppose to be or else feel like you being hung
You can walk or run, but know when it's being done
Don't imagine what they envision, run from it
You'll never find peace there, just pain in your stomach
Don't vomit on the roller coaster of life
Just continue being a man and do things right
I know you waiting on the sun, but its night
Well at least that's what it feels like
Stay strong and keep riding poetry like a bike
If the devil comes near, tell him take a hike
Then start to write, continue to draw
Know your work is awesome, keep thinking about God often
Life itself is a token and let it be something that can't be broken
You strong as ever and still very special
Heart still light as a feather
Words still bring you great weather
When you learn more, you do better
I know you need these words so I'm here to tell them
Everything is ok, pray more than what you do
Let wisdom be your shoes, walk and improve things you feel you should
Keep moving in the manner in which you do
You hard to track, but yet so smooth
Stay under your angel wings, life is such a cruise
Remember I'm under your breath, giving you these thoughts for food

Moments are like . . . . .

Rain drops hitting the top of my house
Wind blowing north and south
A flash a of lighting then thunder open its mouth
I hope homeless ones somewhere dry instead of being out
Traffic lights flickering, power outages in some areas as a tornado siren ring
You know how storms are in the middle of the spring
I'm just letting the pen flow, wet or dry, I do my thing
I can't hold it all in, I record it before it leaves
This how moments are, this not make believe
I'm feeling alone like a single planted seed
It's alright, day in and out that's what I believe
I keep growing to achieve
I have no emotions on my sleeves, just plenty words to read
I'm still drawing on the canvas hours most are sleep
Poems are produced rapidly because my desire create the speed
Heart still beating so I'm still praying on my knees
The rain still coming down, but I feel like it's about to leave
Then the streets smoking because the earth hot and the rain create steam
Living is a miracle witnessed everyday
Your heart beat on a pattern until the sound fade away
Then what happens next?
Well, right now we don't know
The rain has stop so I guess the reason for it is to take it slow
Now the sun coming out so smile with it and glow

$\mathscr{E}$mancipated

I can't stop thinking so I grabbed the pen
Reminiscing about states I've been
In my mind, I mean
I'm still day dreaming anticipating what time will bring
Moments be reflecting my poetry
I've been here before
I wonder if time noticing me?
I'm living among my days of glory,
being prepared to tell my story
All I know is poetry
My art vivid as the wind, present from within
Joy just now starting to settle in,
but only when I'm holding the pen
Only if I could bring those moments through a world of sin
I just made it possible because in your head is where it all begin
I be using mines time and time again
Grateful that it functions like a clock ticking to win
Tick, tock with each stroke of the pen, letting it out,
I can't hold it in if you know what I'm saying
Best insurance for my future is me praying
My thoughts cover lands and my brain is a goldmine
Through life I'm learning how to hold mine
All I'm trying to show is how my soul shines
Day in and out, never in a small amount
I continue to unleash words from my mouth, but silent when I wrote it
These poems be loaded with love, peace, truth and ME
I write what I feel, when I write I feel free

Saving Account

I'm up all alone again
Pen wobbling all around again
Light green in my world my friend
I can't stop, I was born to win
This world torn from sin
God still present like the wind
Heart driven with spectacular images in my head
I'm chasing scenes feeling what I said
Money on my mind like the minute before last
Brakes been pressed in my life, time to hit the gas
Driving fast, but yet cautious of what passes my windshield glass
The world cold and the wind chill make me wonder how long it'll last
Rocket mind state, tomorrow will be a blast
I'm moving at a fine rate gathering my cash
Prophet in disguise fulfilling things that was seen by my eyes
My expressions of life don't contain lies
I won't apologize for how I feel from what I said
Right now, can we pray?
We need that more inside our days so our nights won't chase the graves
Be peaceful and look at God to praise
With all he has given me, why should I have to ask for a raise?
I'll keep cutting these coupons out saving up for my days!

Still Write

I'm still writing despite what anybody think of me
I'm still writing down the site in between the blink of me
I'm still writing because it make me still feel free
I'm still writing a guide to how I be
I'm still writing, I'm still reading
Glory go to God because I'm still writing
I pray for the efforts before me because I'm still fighting
They want to read me because I'm still writing
Blessings still cover me when I'm writing
I'm still writing because lighting keep striking
Rain still pouring but I'm still writing
The sun will shine because I'm still writing
Friction still occur with the devil because I'm still writing
My brain operates better than a computer so I'm still typing
Stumble I might, humble my type which allow me to keep writing
I don't think the outcome will be more fulfilling than the journey that
was born
It all began when I started writing
A prophet in disguise when I'm writing
I conversate with angels and they be telling me keep writing
I'm free at heart and hold beliefs tight as the pen when I'm writing
The wind magical as the moments when I'm writing
You feel it but you didn't see me when I'm writing
Writers block only occur when I don't feel like writing
Which means it never occur because I'm always writing
I'm the physical state of the thoughts I have when I'm writing
A mind is a terrible thing to waste so that's why I'm still writing
In the morning I'll be writing, this afternoon I'll be writing, tonight I'll
be thinking about what I wrote
And my story shall continue like the way I'm holding hope